THE WAY OF THE HR WARRIOR

Leading the **CHARGE**
to Transform Your Career
— and Organization —

THE WAY OF THE
HR WARRIOR

MONICA FREDE & KERI OHLRICH, PhD

Published by
LifeTree Media Ltd.
www.lifetreemedia.com

Distributed by
Greystone Books Ltd.
www.greystonebooks.com

Cataloguing data available from Library and Archives Canada

ISBN 978-1-928055-32-7 (paperback)
ISBN 978-1-928055-33-4 (epub)
ISBN 978-1-928055-34-1 (PDF)

Copyediting: Judy Phillips
Cover and interior design: Naomi MacDougall
Author photos: Jerry Camarillo

Printed and bound in Canada

Distributed in the US by Publishers Group West

To all HR Warriors who are making an impact, big and small, every day in the workplace. We are in this together!

Contents

Charging into the HR Revolution

H ELLO HUMAN RESOURCES professionals!
We are very excited you are reading our book, because we love and respect this profession. HR professionals like yourselves do great work every day. How challenging and rewarding it is! Our combined experiences in HR have led us to believe that the profession can do so much more, and this is why we wrote this book. We want to do what we can to improve our profession so that it makes more of an impact, garners more respect, and is used more wisely in a business setting.

We want to share our personal experiences, along with practical (and, at times, funny) examples of what we've seen work—and not work—in companies. Human Resources is an honorable and altruistic function that has a difficult task: influencing, coaching, encouraging, and advising people to make good choices in the workplace. That's no small task.

How many times have your friends and relatives said "Anyone can work in HR"? We know that statement is simply not true. The rules, the interviews, the rules, the phone calls, the rules... Some days feel anything but "human." As important as rules are, they use up time and energy. And just as important is the strategic work of the HR professional.

Ah, "strategic HR." That's a popular term. Industry conferences, networking events, online blogs, and social media groups all emphasize and promote the strategic work HR can do—and how we must have "a seat at the table."

And yet there are varying ideas about what strategic and nonstrategic work is for an HR professional. A business leader's answer may be very different from that of an HR leader. Why is that? Because of different expectations, based on differing perceptions of what HR can, and should, be doing.

HR focuses efforts on the elements that catalyze a company's success: its employees. No company can flourish without successful employees. HR focuses on hiring the right talent. We focus on training and developing that talent. We focus on keeping that talent. And, when necessary, we focus on excising the wrong talent. People are the soul of any company, and if that soul isn't healthy, the company isn't healthy. From senior leaders to interns, every employee has a hand in shaping the culture of a company. The key to understanding a company today is to determine what its vision is—then you can figure out how you can help achieve it. And HR is in a great position to do just that.

The title of this book, *The Way of the HR Warrior*, refers to two things that may not at first seem like they go together— HR and warriors—but we believe they do. Many HR books offer exceptional information, academic research, business and operating models, and discussions of trends, tactics, and data-driven results. We respect the authors of these books— the HR thought leaders, past and present. And this book does not replace those resources. Rather, it complements them by exploring what makes the foundation of an HR professional—or as we think of it, an HR Warrior. And that foundation we call CHARGE.

The acronym "CHARGE" refers to the key qualities we believe are essential to the HR Warrior: Courage, Humility, Accuracy, Resiliency, Goal-oriented, and Exemplary. In *The Way of the HR Warrior*, you will learn about each quality and how it may or may not be operating in your HR career. Master the CHARGE, and you will accomplish great things for your career and for your organization.

For those of us who are passionate about our work but dismayed at the low expectations and obstructions we encounter from management and other staff, perhaps including our peers in HR, or for those of you who want to work in HR but haven't started yet, read on: this book addresses what we can do to change that negative perception, and it's also clear about what it takes to be an HR Warrior.

In this book, we ask you to evaluate yourself using two assessments. These assessments will help you see how you operate in your profession. How much of an HR Warrior are you? How much of an HR Weenie are you? That last one may sound harsh, but stay with us. We will tell you all about the HR Weenie—at the opposite end of the spectrum from the Warrior—and why, with some work, you don't have to self-identify as one. Then we'll walk you through the six CHARGE qualities, offering you some of our own stories and examples along the way, to spur your creativity and imagination.

We encourage you to make notes throughout this book. Mark it up! Write down any ideas, questions, or creative ways you can bring the qualities of an HR Warrior into your workplace. We understand that your time is valuable. But when an idea hits you, we encourage you to take a few seconds to record it. Your future self will thank you. Taking the time to read this book is an investment in *you*. And that is one investment that will surely pay off in a big way.

We challenge you to take CHARGE of your career. No more sitting on the sidelines, letting the marketplace decide what HR can and cannot accomplish. Let's take CHARGE of the roles we play in our companies. No more settling for job-description-specific work duties. HR can be leveraged in even more significant ways. Let's take CHARGE of the environment around us. We can encourage and inspire our HR partners, and by doing that, we can turn the HR revolution into the HR evolution!

Here is an important consideration to keep in mind as you make your way through this book: we don't have all the answers. This book is a compilation of our collective experience—our successes, as well as our ups and downs and mistakes. And by "mistakes" we don't mean the time the wrong date got filled out on an employment verification form (or I-9, as HR professionals call it). It means advising a senior leader to hire an unknown character, who—shockingly—did some sketchy things in the workplace and cost the company a lot of money. Yikes.

No one is perfect, including the leaders, teams, and industries you work for. But during our careers we have discovered something important: being an HR Warrior is within reach of all HR professionals—if you take the time to build a strong foundation. Yes, it will take a lot of hard work. But you deserve to be an HR Warrior, your company deserves it, and the profession deserves it.

As your HR coaches, we will, through this book, help you create a development plan for your career. We are in HR for the long haul, and refuse to point fingers at a seemingly broken HR function. We are in the fight with you, leading the CHARGE to transform your career, and organization. So let's get started.

Keri and Monica
April 2018

CHAPTER 1

What Is an HR Warrior?

BORING, ADMINISTRATIVE, EASY, stiff, nerdy, police, buzzkill, overhead, party planners, tour guides. Have you ever heard these descriptors used to describe HR? Have you seen how HR is portrayed in the entertainment industry? (As the punch line of a joke, or as dull and uneducated in a script.) Or read articles about how HR needs to be dismantled, redesigned, outsourced, or ignored?

Yes, we have too.

The gap between the negative perception of HR and the truth and reality of our amazing profession is daunting, but we completely believe it can be overcome. Our mission is to see HR become what it's truly meant to be in every company and in every industry—a bunch of stealthy HR Warriors making an impact on their organizations, while developing their careers. All HR professionals have the potential to become Warriors.

So, what exactly is an HR Warrior?

Imagine that employee at work who everyone wants to work with. Whether it's for a new project, a new client, or a new business initiative, everyone wants *them* on the team. So what if they don't work in your department? They get the work done. They know how to stick to deadlines. And they always contribute fresh, inspiring ideas. Maybe they don't have the credentials others do, but they are a great teammate. They exude an air of confidence. That's an HR Warrior.

> The HR Warrior is a professional who can be counted on to get the job done right, to exceed expectations, to inspire others, and to set the expectations that increase the work output of everyone around them. HR Warriors care about what they do. They see their work as an opportunity to have a positive impact on the business every day.

The character of the HR Warrior comprises six indispensable qualities:

Courage
Humility
Accuracy
Resiliency
Goal-oriented
Exemplary

No matter the work environment, no matter the company culture, no matter the internal or external influences, HR Warriors demonstrate these six qualities in a way that lifts the reputation of HR, and challenges the status quo of what it means to work in HR. They have a unique way about them that changes the environment around them. And it happens gradually, day by day, task by task.

In contrast, the HR Weenie wants to perform the minimal amount of work and is not motivated to influence their work environment or to advance the perception of HR. The HR Weenie wants to use the law—federal, state, and local—as the guiding light for all business decisions. The HR Weenie remains distracted, busying themselves with projects, processes, and perceptions, rather than delivering measurable results that have an impact on their peers, other employees, and the company.

An HR Warrior is so much more than a personnel or administrative employee. Becoming one requires more than simply knowing employment law, updating the employee handbook, and speaking verbosely. An HR Warrior is colorful, and doesn't fit the black-and-white definition that has traditionally been used to describe the purpose of Human Resources.

The Ghosts of HR Past

Way back in the day (before any of us were born), the Department of Human Resources was called Personnel Administration: in the United States around the 1920s, the hiring, training, and compensating of employees had become a large enough responsibility that a defined department was needed to manage the human talents of any business. Employees should be viewed as company assets, the theory went.

And companies needed to measure the factors that affected those assets, such as employee safety. Companies needed to establish child labor laws, outline the health impact of industrial working environments, and react to the rise of employee unions, which meant understanding the industrial relations between workers and management.

During the 1970s, employment legislation kicked up into high gear, and Personnel Administration became about keeping the company out of legal trouble. Someone needed to stay on top of new and shifting employment laws and ensure the company was not in violation. In the late 1980s and early 1990s, the workplace began changing again—workplace flexibility and the shift from the traditional employee model with the rise of temporary, contract, and part-time workforces required HR to add employee engagement to their already full plate of responsibilities. Now add technology, predictive analytics, and artificial intelligence (AI)—including robots.

We live in a 24/7 connected world. Employees can work practically anywhere, anytime they choose, thanks to smartphones, laptops, and virtual working environments. Companies have teams of employees located around the world—the new global workforce is a reality. Technology, from applicant tracking systems and performance management tools to automated payroll systems and electronic employee files, has changed the way HR manages their responsibilities; its use is part of a necessary skill set for Human Resources professionals. We've come a long way, baby!

While technology can make our jobs easier, it also presents challenges for the workplace—for instance, as electronic correspondence and remote work increases, knowing how to manage people and having empathy may decrease. And technology evolves more quickly than most of us can keep up with (heck, we can barely keep up with the next smartphone). Finance, sales, and marketing must all adapt to the changing workforce and external forces. Human Resources is no different.

But HR has not transformed fast enough. Far too many employers still refer to our department as the HR Administration Department, or as the HR and Payroll Department. Have you heard of the People and Culture Department? Or the Total Rewards Department? How about the Chief Happiness Officer, Chief People Officer, Talent Specialist, or Diversity and Inclusion Leader? These are actual titles used in actual companies.

We are not slamming these changes. To be honest, holding the title of Chief Happiness Officer would make us smile every day. But HR has a lot more work to do than just change job titles. What HR professionals do every day as they interact with business is what underpins lasting change.

The Perception Gap

Remember the TV show *The Office*? This docu-style show had among its cast of characters an HR manager, Toby Flenderson, whose job was to ask employees to wear appropriate clothing on casual Fridays and who would geek out using the corporate forms to document harassment allegations. In one episode, branch manager Michael Scott is describing his employees as a deck of cards. Toby, he dismissively states, "is the instruction card you throw away."

In the case of many HR professionals, that may not be a stretch. These are the HR managers who function like an instruction manual printed in black and white: Here is what to do and what not to do. They own that employee handbook and have five minutes during each quarterly leadership meeting to reinforce policies and update others on the changes in federal and state employment laws. Yawn. Leadership sees this kind of HR manager as little more than the check-the-box formality in the corporate strategic plan, the person who makes sure the company stays compliant, keeping the company out of the courtroom and flying under the radar of the Equal Employment Opportunity Commission and the Department of Labor.

But for some of you, this characterization does not ring true. You do more than manage compliance or payroll or new-hire documentation. Your tasks are complicated. But that doesn't mean you are operating as an HR Warrior. There may still be much more you can do.

Human Resources has a bad rap today, but this can change—in fact, it's up to you to change it. A revolution starts internally. It starts with the heart, wanting something more meaningful, something that will last, and something that will make our world (our companies) a better place to be.

Human Resources has a bad rap today, **but this can change.**

"A revolution? The heart? Making the world a better place?" you ask, rolling your eyes. And we get it—after all, this is Human Resources we're talking about. We are not preparing to remove the British monarch. But, fellow HR practitioners, changing the perception that the external world, and our business leaders, have of our function can have a profound impact on the way companies operate. And that changes the day-to-day lives of us all.

It's not only television that takes jabs at HR. A notorious *Fast Company* article published in 2005, titled "Why We Hate HR," claimed that "HR people are, for most practical purposes, neither strategic nor leaders."[1] The author continues:

> The human-resources trade long ago proved itself, at best, a necessary evil—and at worst, a dark bureaucratic force that blindly enforces nonsensical rules, resists creativity, and impedes constructive change. HR is the corporate function with the greatest potential—the key driver, in theory, of business performance—and also the one that most consistently underdelivers.

Say it with us: Ou-ch. But is the author of this infamous article wrong? No one wants to be told they need to lose weight. No one wants to hear "Your child is out of control." And no one wants to receive an updated credit report showing the pendulum swinging fully into the red section. The truth hurts. Even if no one is telling you that they see no value in HR, this negative perception is strikingly real, and if it's going to change, it's important to understand why it's so negative.

---

1 Keith H. Hammonds, "Why We Hate HR," *Fast Company*, August 1, 2005, https://www.fastcompany.com/53319/why-we-hate-hr.

A 2015 *Harvard Business Review* issue featured an image of a bomb with a lit fuse on its cover, with the words "It's Time to Blow up HR and Build Something New." A section of the publication was devoted to reinventing HR and included an article titled "Why We Love to Hate HR... and What HR Can Do about It." This article and others were aimed at fixing the HR gap.

The HR gap is really a perception gap. It is the abyss that exists between what companies and their leadership believe we can do and what we know our function can do. On another level, this gap is between what we demonstrate in our daily work and what our business leaders need us to do.

The *Harvard Business Review* article highlights this:

> Usually when companies are struggling with labor issues, HR is seen as a valued leadership partner. When things are going more smoothly all around, managers tend to think, "What's HR *doing* for us, anyway?"[2]

The presence of HR in a company should not treated as dispensable when the executives need to hit their fourth-quarter numbers, only to drop serious change into the training budget in Q1 to binge-hire and develop top talent. We HR professionals need to demonstrate why we are of great value to the business, in good times and bad, because without us, the bad times can be very, very ugly.

Although, in general, plenty of people joke about HR, what about our fellow employees? Inside the company, business leaders undoubtedly (and occasionally unintentionally) show

---

2 Peter Cappelli, "Why We Love to Hate HR... and What HR Can Do about It," *Harvard Business Review*, July-August 2015, 54–61. Emphasis in original.

their disdain for HR. They don't get invited to the grown-ups' Thanksgiving table. They are the teacher's pet who no one wants to talk to at recess. They are the neighbors who residents avoid because they are the watchdogs who call the police when there are loud disturbances after 10 p.m.

We've both felt the pain of the perception gap.

Monica remembers how her business partners often would apologize for comments made during a meeting. "A swear word would slip out, and immediately all eyes would be on me and a heartfelt apology would follow. I remember thinking, 'I'm not writing pink slips . . . I'm here to talk strategy!'"

And Keri recalls walking into a meeting when her colleagues were already seated, biding their time by telling jokes. "They would choke up and apologize as soon as I walked in, as if to say 'HR is in the room and we have to knock it off now.'" That is not how she wanted the leadership team to behave around her, and so she knew she had work to do to change its perception of HR. In another instance, after successfully executing a project with a new team, Keri received this telling compliment: "You aren't like HR at all!"

The theme that emerges is business leaders believe they have HR Weenies working for them. The HR Weenie wants to attend leadership meetings to ensure that someone is present to take notes. The HR Weenie wants to highlight on a spreadsheet the name of every employee who didn't fill out their employment eligibility verification form within three days of hire, and then proudly share this with management. This work has its value—but this isn't the value-added work of an HR Warrior. The HR Warrior must respond to the challenges of today's workforce and workplace by supporting the company's goals while protecting it from itself if necessary.

What is the root of this negative perception? Like an unexpected breakup, you need to ask "What went wrong?" Let's look back to the first date and find out how the relationship with business leaders soured.

Challenges in the Modern Workplace

The workplace has changed. Employee disengagement is a constant concern at the leadership level of any organization. Leaders want to find the magic pill that will improve employee morale. If only it were that easy.

Millennials are working alongside baby boomers, and how each group is engaged in the workplace is as different as their ages. Flexible work options are requested as often as are base pay increases. While most managers are looking for ways to cut costs, high-profile companies are adding petting zoos and Zen gardens complete with meditation spaces. Employees want to work from home, work in open workspaces, or work in balanced workspaces.

No one is paid enough for the work they do—if only they were paid an extra $12,000 per year, they would be engaged. But they are put off until the next merit season. Everyone wants a full match from the employer for their retirement savings plan. They want more benefits, lower out-of-pocket costs, better coverage. This is why the compensation and benefits team bears the full brunt of low ratings during employee survey season.

And then there are external challenges that keep the top-level executives, aka the C-suite, up at night. Have you heard of this little thing called the Internet of Things (IoT)? This term refers to the influence of technology in our connected world. Technology continues to reshape the global economy by reshaping the way business is done. That smartphone in your hand? It can run our lives. That ATS system? It can categorize thousands upon thousands of eligible job seekers with "unique" skills and abilities. That smartwatch? It can explain why you are so cranky come three o'clock (sleep more!). Data analytics is on the rise, including behavioral analytics. Businesses must keep up with changing technologies and changing employees.

IoT is changing the way we use products and services, interact with people and businesses, and create careers. Automation, artificial intelligence, drones, and kiosks are replacing jobs in fast-food restaurants, retail stores, and car dealerships. This conjures up the dreaded "o" word. Outsourcing is the ugly topic whispered about in the breakroom, and it's threatening the jobs of tenured employees and recent college graduates alike. Quick and cheap labor, along with reduced overhead costs such as health benefits, appeals to stockholders and the board of directors, but is terrifying to employees. Increasingly, work can be done through automation and by robots, including reviewing résumés and conducting phone interviews with candidates using predetermined questions. For employees, the new workplace can be scary.

The temptation to outsource North American jobs is real. The temptation to bring in cheaper labor to take the seats of North American workers is also real. North American workers know this, and it can lead to fear, which can lead to a disengaged workforce.

Once again, enter the need for HR Warriors.

Leaders walk the fine line between town hall conversations with employees and answering to the board of directors.

Cutting costs by all means necessary while still getting the employee base excited about the company's future is a challenge for any leader. Messaging is an important executive responsibility, and HR needs to understand the messages from leadership and help translate them for employees. HR sees the business from both sides—the employer's and the employee's; in between, however, is room for a lot of confusion, misunderstanding, and assumption.

The 2014 Global Workforce Study by Willis Towers Watson found that 70 percent of employees feel their company should understand them just as much as the employees are expected to understand their clients, but only 43 percent of employees feel this is the case. The study also identified three sustainable and measurable elements that significantly impact an employee's desire to stay with their employer: traditional engagement, enablement, and energy provided through the workplace. The survey found that only 40 percent of employees felt that these three elements were in sufficient force to keep them highly engaged.[3]

Only 40 percent! The term "employee engagement" is quite the buzzkill since the very mention of it elicits appendicitis-like pain for anyone in the C-suite.

When in the ring with employee engagement, company leadership faces a tough opponent. HR should be in the ring too, but we are too busy updating the attendance policy. We should be in lockstep with the shift in desirable qualities of human capital, but we are buried beneath regulations and benefits administration—or maybe we choose to bury

---

3 Willis Towers Watson, "2014 Global Workforce Study at a Glance," https://www.towerswatson.com/assets/jls/2014_global_workforce_study_at_a_ glance_emea.pdf.

ourselves in the rules, preferring to act like an ostrich in the sand. The time has come for HR to shift from thinking about rules to thinking about values.

And, speaking of rules, one more pressure on executives is the impact of business regulations. The National Association of Manufacturers calculates that federal regulations cost small companies (those with fewer than fifty employees) almost $12,000 per employee each year.

Yes, the administrative tasks that fall within your job description are important, but increased regulations are an opportunity for HR to find creative, workable solutions that mean much more to a company than simply keeping it in compliance.

We are in a new era of business called the knowledge economy and where growth is increasingly tied to information rather than to a means of production. Companies are placing high value on intellectual capital, the intangible assets of their employees. Multigenerational workforces, increasing competition for labor, and increasing regulations that have an impact on business decisions—all are factors that come into play as companies pursue profits and capitalize on business opportunities by harnessing their human capital.

If that weren't enough, members of a young and powerful generation, the millennials, are currently building their careers, with Gen Zers right on their heels. Deloitte, Gallup, and IBM's Institute for Business Value have all surveyed millennials and discovered that what they want is for their company to not only pursue profits but be a force for positive societal change, and to provide a workplace that offers perks such as remote work options and flexibility for work-life balance.

Business leaders rely on HR to help with these important matters, but they want more from us. HR Warriors want to do more as well. We want to change the landscape of an organization, and we want to tackle challenging issues impacting the morale and engagement of employees.

Employee engagement has a significant impact on a company's success. The happier employees are at work, the more productive they are, and the more the company benefits. Think of the Seven Dwarfs happily singing each morning on the assembly line. Maybe employees won't sing, but they can be happy during the forty-plus hours they spend at work.

How do we keep employees happy and engaged at work? That's the million-dollar question. And every leader wants the answer to it, and wants the help of HR to answer it. In fact, they are blatantly crying out for help, because human capital is the most potent force in any company. The business landscape will not become less competitive any time soon, meaning a winning team will help the company win.

Human Resources must intimately understand, interact with, and influence human beings—from intern to C-suite. This is a big responsibility, and an even greater opportunity, because people are complicated. They're the wild card in the workplace. The catalyst for conquering the competition. And the people arena is the arena in which HR Warriors shine.

Life is unpredictable. An employee can go home at the end of the workweek and before they pull their car back into the employee parking lot on Monday morning—drastic events may have occurred in their life. The beloved family dog may have died. Maybe they had a fight with a friend or partner. Or their child broke his foot during Saturday's soccer game and the follow-up doctor's appointment is scheduled for the same time as the all-important quarterly review with a client.

Personal lives bleed into the workplace constantly, and Human Resources can bridge the gap between what the company needs from their employees and what the employee needs for their own well-being.

Oftentimes, leadership does not recognize HR's potential to positively impact the bottom line. Or leadership isn't confident in HR's ability to influence the workplace. Ouch. And sometimes, leadership doesn't want HR to influence the workplace—they want HR to submit payroll in time and update the handbook once a year. Double ouch.

A Contributing Partner

There is a Chinese proverb that says "The best time to plant a tree was twenty years ago. The second-best time is now."

Now is the time to plant the tree of a talented, strategic, strong, powerful Human Resources department. Because, as HR professionals, we can be influencers, even game changers, in the business landscape. We can fortify the bridge between employee and leadership, and we can close the perception gap between leadership and HR. But to be an effective HR business partner, you must walk in the shoes of the company leadership.

New competition, new purpose, and a new brand are no easy tasks for a leader to effectively manage. And the challenges keeping leaders up at night should keep HR up also.

Companies have an opportunity to differentiate themselves from their competitors, and you and the leadership should be able to describe what you do that is better—for employees, for the community, and for the world. Some companies have woven their authenticity into their brand to great effect. Herein lies an opportunity for Human Resources: to

As HR professionals, we can be influencers, **even game changers, in the business landscape.**

drive the leadership team to define and articulate a corporate mission that means more than profits, and create an employee value proposition to attract talent that can fulfill that mission.

Be realistic about what it takes to elevate your HR game. It's common to hear attendees at Human Resource conferences talk about how HR must own one of the coveted "seats at the table." This means that HR would attend the top-level meetings and be part of discussions and decisions made by the biggest players of a company. Agreed. That's absolutely a table that HR should be sitting at. We should be breaking bread with the C-suite. Make sure that you get the invite.

But having a seat at the table doesn't mean that chair is reserved for you and you alone. You need to prove that the seating plan is incomplete without you and your contribution. When you have the foundation for success, you are invaluable in driving the business forward. Yet, having that chair reserved simply because the company needs you is not good enough. You need to carve HR's name on that chair, to show it's a permanent member of the brainstorming team, the leadership team, the team that gets work done. Being this kind of essential strategic business partner is what we mean by the phrase "Be an HR Warrior."

Companies need HR. And they need you to do more than process payroll. Leaders are facing daunting challenges both internally and externally. When it comes to business, it's survival of the fittest, no matter a company's maturation or mission. Leadership needs HR, even if they don't yet realize it. That's where you come in: you can show leadership what HR Warriors do, and how your work is indispensable to achieving the mission.

We have already made the point that HR should be "strategic." An increasingly common job title and one that aligns with this adjective is "HR business partner" (or HRBP, as the cool kids say). But what exactly does this all mean? Whole books have been written about what it means; read up on the latest theories in your spare time!

Meanwhile, here's an extremely condensed explanation: a strategic business partner is someone who has moved beyond an administrative role and is perceived as a valued partner who contributes to complex business objectives and drives results. And that's an HR Warrior.

Polar opposite of the problem-solving guru who works closely with leadership to address the significant challenges facing the company is the HR professional who participates only in transactional work that has an immediate impact on employees and management. That's an HR Weenie.

Which do you want to be? Which does your organization need you to be?

It's Not about the Job Title

The way to transform HR is not by changing our job title. As mentioned, people are transforming the HR job title into new and creative ones, Chief Happiness Officer, Chief People Officer, and Chief Talent Officer among them. A few of these title changes are really just companies putting a different dust jacket on the same book. However, in other cases, these title changes do represent a significant transformation of the HR leader's role. Yes, our focus is on changing the story, but rebranding doesn't necessarily revamp a reputation; it's the work that happens daily that does.

The focus of HR should be transforming into a business-first team, led by leaders and practitioners who are on the front lines of driving corporate strategy through employees. HR translates the goals of the leaders into what the employees do every day. After all, a return on investment in people is a return on investment for the business.

A name can do only so much to change the perception of what HR does, and what its persona is. If you get married and change your last name, great. But that usually doesn't change who you are or how you behave. What HR needs to do to see true transformation is change the way leadership sees us, and what they ask us to do.

Let us say that again: we need to change what leadership asks us to do.

- Does leadership ask you to create a talent strategy for the upcoming year that will directly impact the bottom line?

- Does your front-line management team ask you to address the high turnover in a technical position, which is resulting in reduced productivity?

- Does leadership ask you for ideas on creating the optimal structure to drive business for the future?

These are the kinds of questions you want to hear from leadership. If, instead, you are asked during the leadership summit if you would refill the coffee pot, you might be an HR Weenie.

What *are* you asked to do? Take thirty seconds to think about this. Recall your last week of work. Recall what you did at the end of last year to prepare for the upcoming year. Recall the last leadership meeting you attended and who in the room addressed you, and what they asked. If it was only about payroll, personnel files, or perks in the workplace, you've got a perception gap.

Leadership should be asking you to handle complex and strategic problems that those in the corner offices must deal with every single day. You are a part of the company strategy, and the work you do has a direct impact on the company's success.

Employees are any company's greatest asset. How employees do their work is what makes a company function, successfully or not. It works the same way in sports, in community organizations, in relationships. The old saying "What you give is what you get" is true.

HR is immensely important to the way employees under-stand their abilities, value their role, and perceive their daily work. That's a big responsibility! An even greater respon-sibility for HR is showing the leadership team that we are immensely valuable to achieving the company goals.

It's time to close the perception gap. View this as an oppor-tunity, rather than as a problem. Ironically, when clients or business partners hold resentful feelings towards HR, it's a promising starting point. A psychology professor of Keri's once said that he wanted to work with kids who were angry, because they have hope; the kids who don't care are the hardest ones to help. So let's use that negative energy to our advantage. We have the most to gain by fixing what's broken.

The Nature of Transformation

Do you want to become an HR Warrior? Do you want to do transformational work, and realize the potential in the HR role, even if leadership doesn't see it? That takes nothing short of a transformation, and any transformation takes time, dedi-cation, and consistency. The focus should not be to buy real estate in Wishville. Make a serious commitment to growth and keep the Warrior vision in front of you. Don't just wish for more—do more.

You would not be reading this if you didn't want more for yourself and your career. This book is a guide on how to trans-form your career and, more importantly, your organization. Focus on values, not rules; ignore your leadership's lack of expectation and show them you have the qualities of a kickass HR Warrior!

We can already hear you saying, "All this sounds well and good, but management would never go for that" or "I used to feel that optimistic on the job . . . " or "If only there were room for me to be an HR Warrior, but all anyone lets me be is a paper pusher." We know it's somewhat of a catch-22 situation. To be an HR Warrior requires permission and empowerment from leadership, but until you exhibit your true relevance, power, and potential as an HR Warrior, leadership will sideline you.

You can't control what leadership does. What you can control is what you do. Focus on your own qualities and behavior. Do your best to handle resistance well but don't wait on the sidelines. Avoid defensiveness, and as much as you can, don't allow yourself to be diminished. All this said, it's important to recognize when your work environment is unhealthy and you might need to consider leaving—something we talk about in Chapter 9.

You may feel a little HR Weenie-ish right now, and that's okay. Be like those angry kids. Recognize that if you are reading this book, you expect more out of yourself. The next chapter will help you identify your current state, and help you build a blueprint for personal development. The revolution begins within—and you are on the way!

CHAPTER 2

Looking in the HR Mirror

ARE YOU READY to be an HR Warrior? Yes? Great! In Chapter 1, we provided the definition of "Warrior" and of "Weenie." Now it's time to walk through how to be a Warrior. But first you need to assess how much of one you are already.

It can be difficult to assess ourselves accurately. Looking in the mirror works well for, well, seeing our superficial appearance. But what do our behaviors, motivations, and passions look like? Determining that can be a little more challenging, but by placing a "mirror" in front of your heart and mind, you'll be off to a good start. This chapter requires an honest self-assessment, and that won't be easy. However, the tools provided here will help make the process a little less painful. It's not about what you would like to identify with, or what you used to identify with; it's about your current state—it's knowing where you stand today. If you want to take a road trip to California, first you enter your starting point—your home address—into your GPS. The assessment tools in this chapter will help you determine your "home address" on the HR Warrior map. It's time to be brutally honest with yourself.

Behavioral Anchors

In Chapter 1, we explained that an HR Warrior is an individual who is transforming the image of HR through daily personal commitments to achieve excellence. It's these daily personal commitments that we call Warrior behavioral anchors. "Behavioral anchor" sounds a lot like what it is: a behavior that anchors someone, either positively or negatively. Anchors can keep a person in the same spot in their career, or function like a strong mooring so that they can weather all storms.

The list of anchors below is based on personal experiences—our own and that of our fellow HR partners. These anchors are not scientifically researched, university-proofed, or adaptations of ancient methodology. We've worked in organizations that utilize HR in different ways, and we've felt the pain of being both underused and overextended—thus, we identified the anchors by doing a gut check. Use them to determine the behaviors you need to embrace in order to kick-start the HR Warrior within. They are meant to help you gauge your current state as you start on the self-assessments.

HR Warrior Behavioral Anchors

A popular American reality TV show called *American Ninja Warrior* is exactly what you would expect it to be: modern-day gladiators with ripped muscles, stone-cold stares, and brute strength akin to Greek gods pounding through an obstacle course. They may be warriors in terms of physical ability, but they are not exactly accurate representations of those in an HR career. The TV warriors can be intimidating, but an HR Warrior is not. We are, however, an inspiration. If you are an HR Warrior, you exhibit these anchoring behaviors:

- **Working for the win:** Even if the C-suite and leadership don't like HR, you work with them anyway. Over time, you show what HR can do for them and for the company.

- **Exhibiting brutal honesty:** Sometimes it's necessary to give hard feedback, whether to a leader, coworker, or manager. You do so for the betterment of the team.

An HR Warrior is transforming the image of HR **through daily personal commitments to achieve excellence.**

- **Engaging with crisis:** You do not shy away from a crisis but get pumped at the opportunity to solve a critical or massive problem. You are visible to your business partners, in both good times and bad.

- **Displaying curiosity:** You ask a lot of great questions, and the questions are not for your benefit but to obtain a deep understanding of the issues, concerns, and needs of the business, and to be a proactive business partner.

- **Learning constantly:** You love learning. Reading, studying, asking questions, and remaining involved in the industry is what you do without being told to.

- **Speaking plainly:** You avoid "HR speak," because the goal is not to confuse business partners but to speak the same language.

- **Listening with two ears:** Most of your conversations with employees and partners are spent listening. Questions have a time and a place, and that time is usually later.

- **Acting with agility:** You remain proactive, flexible, and adaptable to business changes in order to support your leadership in the challenging decisions they've made.

- **Remaining steady like a rock:** Emotions are in the workplace and you are not immune. But you can acknowledge them and still accomplish your goals.

- **Never giving up:** After being knocked down, you get back up. Regardless of mistakes or mini failures, you see your career and the impact you are making within the big picture.

- **Staying the course:** No matter what others may say about you,

you respond with kindness to everyone and focus on achieving your goals.

- **Belonging to the achiever's club:** Even if plans take longer than expected to come to fruition, you don't give up on those goals. You adjust and continue to work towards completion.

- **Enjoying problem-solving:** You have a demonstrated history of getting results. Problems are meant to be solved, and you do exactly that.

- **Measuring activity:** You can demonstrate to the company metrics-based results and quantifiable activities that align with the goals of the business.

- **Considering the numbers first:** When designing solutions, the numbers come first. Can you measure your results for the business? What is most important for the business?

- **Believing in the long game:** Not all solutions have to be an immediate win. You keep in mind the long-term goals of the business and the employee base, and help your business partners make wise decisions that are for the betterment of the team and the organization in the long term.

- **Showing, not telling:** You include your business partners in the process and share ownership of great results. Teamwork for the win!

- **Sharing what you know:** Caring is sharing. Whether for your HR colleagues, the business, or even people outside your organization, you have a desire to see everyone in HR excel.

- **Building trust:** HR must be a trustworthy business partner, and you have developed that reputation. The more trustworthy you are, the more opportunities that will arise for you to be a part of the business.

Got all that? Now let's look at the behavioral anchors that show up in a Weenie.

HR Weenie Behavioral Anchors

It sounds harsh to call one of our own a Weenie. No offense meant. This list of behavioral anchors could prove painful if you acknowledge any of them in yourself. Remember that self-awareness is the first step in knowing what direction you want to go. Be okay with being brutally honest with yourself. It's short-term pain for the long-term win. Do you recognize any of these behaviors in yourself as an HR professional?

- **Missing the mark:** You do not deliver on time. You are always missing deadlines, goals, and the target.

- **Resisting change:** You prefer not to change the systems currently in place, because that can be risky and also requires adjusting how you do your work.

- **Being a Negative Nancy:** Anytime a new idea is proposed, you have a reason it cannot be done.

- **Seeing the law as your BFF:** It is the answer to anything and everything fellow employees ask you.

- **Being ER reactive:** You do not discover employee relations (ER) issues; employees come to you via email or phone.

- **Faking the positive:** You want the appearance of perfection, and employ the "Everything is awesome" approach, regardless of the situation or audience.

- **Design paralysis:** You cannot decide on your goals or a program strategy, or are constantly redesigning them, preventing the business from installing the finished product.

- **Speaking first and never holding your peace:** In a feedback or listening session, you often answer quickly and before others can raise questions.

- **Using "no" as a reflex:** You say no, followed by "because … " to quickly close down discussion and halt progress.

- **Believing in conflict:** You believe that business leaders and HR do not have the same goals, and that the business goals conflict with HR's goals.

- **Acting as the police officer:** The police have arrived. The compliance police, the employee handbook police, and the politeness police, that is, and they participate in every meeting.

- **Playing the blame game:** You believe that a bad judgment or bad decision always originates outside the realm of HR.

- **Preferring to get along:** Regardless of what employees or leaders say or do, you agree wholeheartedly. You place emphasis on getting along and being liked, rather than taking a hit to your reputation for all the right reasons.

If you saw elements of your own behavior in this list, this is not a call to quit the profession because clearly you have chosen the wrong career path. Not at all! Although some HR Weenies often want to stay HR Weenies, this does not mean they don't have the ability to change. You *can* develop into an HR Warrior, but to do so, you must first decide that you want to change. You are an HR Weenie only if you choose to be.

With your bright future in mind, we have created two assessment tools to help you determine your current state. The first is the HR Weenie-to-Warrior Assessment, which will help you assess how close (or how far) you are from Warrior status. The second tool is the Organizational Assessment. No one works in a vacuum. Many factors influence how we do our jobs, and to some extent, how effective we are. The Organizational Assessment will help you consider those external factors on your ability to become a Warrior. But first, let's talk about you.

HR Weenie-to-Warrior Assessment

The HR Weenie-to-Warrior Assessment involves a series of statements to be rated on a scale of 1 to 5, where a 1 means it does not describe you and your experience today at all and 5 means it describes you perfectly. Here are the rating options broken down:

1 = Never/not at all.
2 = Not as often as I would like, but occasionally I do this.
3 = Sometimes/about half the time.
4 = This is my goal, but I don't always reach it.
5 = Yes! Proud to say I do this consistently and am known for it.

Record your rating for each of the statements below on a piece of paper or on this page of the book. Remember, this is a chance to be brutally honest with yourself. No one other than you will see your ratings. (You'll read below how to gauge your score).

1. You work with people who don't like HR, but you find a way to partner with them and accomplish great things anyway.

2. You deliver difficult feedback to employees or coworkers when necessary, no matter how uncomfortable it may be.

3. You get asked to take on projects that will be time-consuming, challenging, and emotional.

4. When you attend a team or department meeting, you make it a point to ask at least one quality question in front of the group.

5. You have a career mentor at work or in another company who you talk to routinely.

6. You communicate in a way that would allow any employee to understand complex situations in simple terms.

7. When employees ask to speak with you to share concerns, they do most of the talking.

8. You pivot and change course as necessary because of an important shift in business priority.

9. You remain stoic in the face of emotionally charged situations (even if later you need to cry or yell in the bathroom stall or go for a long walk after work to cool down).

10. You choose to learn from mistakes, instead of giving up on yourself.

11. When you receive negative or hurtful feedback, you find a way to press on towards your goals and respond with gratitude.

12. You have career goals that are going in a different direction, or are taking far longer to achieve than you thought, but you still are taking actionable steps to achieve them.

13. Each of your tasks has a clear, specific goal attached to it.

14. You are able to explain to a business leader how the tasks that you do apply directly to a business objective.

15. You are able to describe the return on investment (ROI) you achieved of your goals within the last twelve months.

16. You read career- or industry-related publications outside of work.

17. You have taken an opportunity to mentor a new employee, or teach something new to a fellow employee.

18. You hear from business partners that you are trustworthy.

Once you've rated all eighteen statements, total the individual ratings, then use the score chart below to determine where you are today on the Weenie-to-Warrior spectrum (a description of each category follows).

18–42: HR Weenie
43–67: HR Wishful
68–90: HR Warrior

HR Weenie

It appears that you have areas to improve on and some decisions to make. Falling in the zone of 18–42 does not mean you need to change careers. It doesn't mean you cannot succeed as an HR Warrior. It simply means that you are, right now, an HR Weenie. But with personal commitment, hard work, and a blueprint for success, this will change. Keep reading!

HR Wishful

If you scored in the zone of 43-67, you fall into a category we haven't yet introduced, the HR Wishful. This category essentially recognizes that life isn't always straightforward and easy. Some days may feel like a total fail. Life is a continual spectrum of change. This is both bad news and great news. The bad news is that you've got work to do. The great news is that you get to improve! Scoring as an HR Wishful means you are aware of the work that lies ahead to become a Warrior. In some areas, you feel strong. In others, not so much. But you have the desire and the will to achieve more, and you have a vision for what you want to be.

HR Warrior

Congratulations! You are already exhibiting a great deal of Warrior power in your career. The most important thing you can do now as an HR Warrior is to keep growing. As we define each CHARGE quality, identify opportunities to continue growing and enhancing your success. We encourage you to review the statements you feel point to where more work on your part is required and focus on ways to improve.

Before you spend too much time thinking about your Warrior, Wishful, or Weenie status, consider three important facts:

1. The total score ratings are based on our years of experience (we are not survey scientists). It describes the place you are at *today*—it is not static.

2. Regardless of your score, we can all improve. Stay encouraged!

3. The environment in which you work can have an impact on the way you answered your questions.

Organizational Assessment

No department, especially HR, is an island. We cannot show up for work, stay in our cubicle, enter data into a spreadsheet, and go home at the end of the day. We are *human* resources. We interact with people, and people are unpredictable. Our environment also is unpredictable.

For example, what if your company wants HR to only do administrative work, and it chooses to outsource strategic work to a consultant? Or what if you work within an HR department that has a VP who lacks direction, discipline, or a desire to advance the team? What if the company was recently acquired by another larger firm that will now blend two very diverse HR teams into one?

External circumstances can be outside your control, and you should consider those influences when assessing your HR Warrior status. In other words, it may be difficult to shine like an HR Warrior if the organization you work for won't let you. The following is a list of possible challenges in the workplace. Do any of these sound familiar?

- The HR budget is slashed, and only "essential" HR roles such as HR generalist are retained. Other roles, like those involving talent and organization development, have been reduced.

- The HR budget doesn't allow for training, in-person meetings, or development programs.

- The clients of HR do not want any involvement beyond administrative tasks such as processing payroll and new-hire paperwork.

- Employee relations issues, including investigations, are handled solely at the management level, and HR is informed only of the results and impending decisions.

- The company has engaged in new partnerships to outsource many HR functions.

- The ratio of HR generalist to employees effectively is too large. HR cannot be successful when supporting hundreds of clients.

- The HR Department has too many layers, or too few layers, minimizing the role individuals can play.

- The HR leader isn't supportive of or doesn't believe in the need to develop the department into a proactive, strategic partner with the business.

If you experience any of these detractors, we are not here to say you should quit your job. Nor do we advise storming into the corner office or confronting an executive in the cafeteria and forcing them to agree you should be an HR Warrior. Instead, consider carefully how your workplace environment is a factor in what you can accomplish in your role.

If you scored at the low end on the HR Weenie-to-Warrior Assessment, recognize that sometimes a workplace constrains the HR-Warrior-in-the-making. The Organizational Assessment involves a series of statements that can help you determine the challenges in your workplace environment. The rating system is similar to that of the first assessment, but the statements are about your organization, rather than about you. Rate each statement on how much your organization does or does not participate in said behavior. Here is the rating scale:

1 = Never/not at all.

2 = Not as often as the company should, but occasionally it does.

3 = Sometimes/about half the time.

4 = This is the company's goal, but it doesn't always reach it.

5 = Yes! Proud to say my company does this consistently and is known for it.

Record your rating for each of the statements below on a piece of paper or on this page of the book. (You'll learn below how to gauge your score.)

1. Your organization fully funds the plans and strategies of the HR Department.

2. Your organization has outsourced nonstrategic, administrative work of HR, so that the internal HR team can focus on the strategic work.

3. Your organization has a diverse organizational chart for HR that includes Talent, Organization Development, Inclusion, and Wellness.

4. Your organization makes it easy for you to keep administrative tasks to a minimum.

5. You are able to easily empower the managers you work with to address issues of compliance with their employees.

6. Managers and employees feel comfortable talking with you.

7. Your client or business partner relies on you for advice.

8. You are able to perform your job without taking shortcuts.

9. Your organization works with you to hire the best candidates possible.

10. You are allowed to be proactive when coming up with creative solutions and to operate with a level of autonomy when the company requires guidance in HR matters.

11. The HR leadership asks for feedback and/or an NPS (net promoter score) from business partners to assess the success of HR.

12. Your organization encourages your curiosity and pursuit of additional training opportunities.

13. Your business colleagues consider you a partner and include you in meetings and important decisions at the same level as your counterparts in other departments.

14. During business hours, you spend most of your time meeting with employees and leaders, and a minimum of time at your desk.

15. Your organization reliably meets its own deadlines and frowns upon a culture of continual catch-up.

16. In times of trouble, your organization mobilizes to find solutions.

17. Your organization constantly revisits its vision for growth, to avoid being stuck in a rut.

18. Your passion for work is regularly met or exceeded by coworkers and management.

19. If you make a mistake, management gives you the time and opportunity to find a solution without consequence.

20. Your organization takes an active and involved role in hiring the best talent for HR.

Now it's time to tally your responses. Use the score chart below to determine to what extent your organization helps or hinders your ability to develop into an HR Warrior (a description of each category follows).

20–40: HR Problem
41–70: HR Potential
71–100: HR Promoter

HR Problem

This is an organization that has numerous institutional barriers in place that inhibit HR Warriors in the workplace. These barriers could be the result of budget constraints, leadership style, the strategic focus of the company and the HR team, the expectations of HR, or bias as to what HR can accomplish.

HR Potential

This is an organization that has found value in HR beyond managing personnel. There is light at the end of the tunnel for your organization to fully support an adept, multifaceted, all-encompassing HR function and achieve company greatness!

HR Promoter

The company truly gets what HR can do. This vision stems from the most senior leadership and is felt all the way through to the employee population. HR is critical to the success of the company, and is an indispensable business partner, with a great deal of responsibility.

REGARDLESS OF YOUR SCORE, don't declare your organization's status on social media! Instead, consider where you stand individually (as HR Warrior, HR Wishful, or HR Weenie) and what level of influence you believe your company has on your status (HR Problem, HR Potential, HR Promoter).

The Overall Picture

This chart will help you visualize how much the work environment and your development overlap to impact progress towards HR Warrior.

	WEENIE	WISHFUL	WARRIOR
PROMOTER	Study	Budding Love	Love
POTENTIAL	Study	Growth	Budding Love
PROBLEM	Stuck	Frustration	Frustration

- **Stuck:** This is a problem. You have much development to do, but your work environment will not allow for it. If you really want to achieve the status of HR Warrior, it may be time to consider if you are working for the right company.

- **Frustration:** Something isn't right, and you can both feel it and see it. This is a challenging situation, one that will require courage on your part if you're going to become an HR Warrior. You will also need to have a serious conversation with yourself about whether your current organization has the capacity to move into a Potential or Promoter state.

- **Study:** The environment in which you work will be helpful to you as you grow towards HR Warrior status. Leverage the resources and opportunities within your company to develop.

- **Growth:** You are on your way! The kind of work environment you are working in is conducive to the creation of an HR Warrior. Stay consistent and keep making progress.

- **Budding love:** The work environment and your career are learning to work together and achieve great results. Don't let up on the gas pedal—keep CHARGE-ing ahead!

- **Love:** Things are wonderful, because you are in a company that values the contribution of an HR Warrior, and you've made great strides to function as one. It may be time to consider how you can help others achieve this level of success.

The statements in this Organizational Assessment are designed to give you an idea of how much the workplace environment hinders or helps your pathway to HR Warrior. Review your score on the personal assessment next to your score on the workplace assessment, to see how similar or dissimilar they are.

Whether your organization finds itself HR Warrior-friendly or HR Warrior-antagonistic, the following chapters put the focus on you. Remember the six essential qualities of the HR Warrior identified in the Introduction?

Courage
Humility
Accuracy
Resiliency
Goal-oriented
Exemplary

You'll have noticed that, together, the first letter of each spells out the word "charge." We want to help you take CHARGE of your career and find opportunities to better yourself, those you work with, and your organization.

CHARGE

CHAPTER 3
C Is for Courage

"MERRY CHRISTMAS AND HAPPY HOLIDAYS! You're fired." Far too many employees have heard lines like this. The fourth quarter arrives, and companies need to adjust before the calendar year closes. CEOs have bottom lines, and investors and shareholders to respond to; sales were not as strong as predicted, the marketing strategy yielded pale results, the new product fell faster than a bowling ball on a seesaw. An unfortunate fix to dismal sales figures can be laying off employees.

HR is right in the midst of all this when it happens; indeed, Keri has been present during many of these October conversations. As an HR leader for a US-based division, Keri urged the leadership team to adjust the employee reduction timeline. "We should do it by the end of October, or wait until January" was her staunch standpoint. "We cannot inform people one week before Thanksgiving that they will lose their job one week before Christmas. What a horrible experience!" She wanted to present leadership with multiple options for the timing of layoffs and consider the employees' points of view. "When would you want to be told?" she asked.

The "horrible experience" was a significant con on the pros and cons list, but one that, after days of passionate debate, continued to be ignored. The leadership team, led by the head of Finance, had to reduce a segment of the population and had no other option. Keri accepted this but was fighting for a new timeline. Do the reductions quickly in October, she suggested, or push them off until January, and we won't ruin hundreds of holidays. But the team had the timeline built: announcements one week before Thanksgiving.

Keri went back to the Finance leader again. "Think like an employee," she advised. "When would you want to be told?" When the leader asked, "What is the business reason?," Keri stated the obvious: because it's the right thing to do. But the leader didn't capitulate. She tried a third time—for the sake of their holidays, for the sake of their families—please do it now or hold on to the announcement. But to no avail: announcements would be made just days before Thanksgiving.

Realizing that she did not win this fight, Keri turned her attention to how the communications would take place. "We will build a communication plan that will notify the employees as quickly as possible, and I recommend we offer to pay them through January 2." The leader agreed. Even though she lost the holiday war, Keri won a battle.

COURAGE IS NOT EASY to come by. But instead of wishing for courage, like the Cowardly Lion in *The Wizard of Oz*, Warriors build this quality over time and through experience. In this chapter, we explore why Warriors need to be courageous, and what it means to show courage:

- Warriors do not take the easy way out. A willingness to do what others will not takes courage. Courage takes effort!

- Not everyone is going to love you. You will have enemies and frenemies. Be okay with that.

- Don't be afraid to go toe to toe with leadership. You are a partner, not a leadership pawn. Speak up, even if you are concerned for your job. This may be scary, but you will sleep better at night knowing you spoke up for yourself.

Courage Takes Effort

What is something you are afraid of? Heights? Spiders? Airplanes? The interesting thing about fears is that it's usually not the object or situation itself that we are afraid of but the consequences of encountering it. Someone who is afraid of heights is afraid of falling. Spiders are relatively inoffensive, but some have a nasty bite. And though airplanes are still a safe way to travel, some people are still afraid they might crash.

Fear leads us to think about what *could* happen, but what if nothing bad happens at all? Courage overcomes the fear of the unknown. Courage is to have a plan, a strategy of even the smallest steps, designed to accomplish goals despite fear. And sometimes having courage means acting even when you are afraid.

Feel the fear and do it anyway. HR Warriors embody courage. They don't play it safe.

Even if you have never spoken in public, you as an HR Warrior take the opportunity to lead a new-hire orientation class. You might be afraid you'll buckle under the pressure—with all those eyes upon you, all those people questioning whether you are truly an expert—but you lead the class anyway.

Warriors prepare for the class. They watch other leaders speak in front of groups. They review company information, become intimately familiar with the history, the key statistics, the philosophy of the company so that they are prepared to answer any question. They do their homework! And even when they get up in front of the room, with everyone looking at them, they may still feel nauseated. That's okay. Each time you lead a class it gets a little easier, and you may feel a little less sick to your stomach.

Demonstrating courage in the workplace takes effort. It doesn't take any effort to show up for a scheduled interview as your organization searches for a replacement VP of Sales and go through the motion of asking the same old questions:

- Why did you leave your last organization?
- Where do you see yourself in five years?
- What interests you about this role?

Sure, you can gather a few key details and enough information in order to provide a thumbs-up or thumbs-down for the interview panel. The executive team will give you a nod of approval, completely underwhelmed by your input.

Or you can go the extra mile.

HR Warriors review the candidate's résumé in detail, taking notes about roles and responsibilities that stand out, in full preparation for an hour-long conversation. During interviews, HR Warriors ask open-ended questions, followed by three "why" questions, to dig deep into a candidate's philosophy:

- Why do you think you exceeded your sales quota at Jade International? (The candidate explains that she added more new accounts than any other sales managers.)

- Why do you think you were able to build a larger portfolio than all the other sales managers? (Because I have a great prospecting process, she says.)

- Why is your prospecting process so successful?

And so on.

Drill down, dig deep, and put in real effort to present an intensive, detailed summary of the candidate to the executive team. The leadership team will take notice of your commitment to the process. Warriors do not take the easy way out, and their organization—and clients—are better for it. Do not let fear keep you from committing 100 percent to the process.

DURING OUR CAREERS, we both have built and executed a fair number of communication plans. These plans are used to manage the internal messages shared with employees—the what, when, and how—when a significant change happens within an organization. Many times, HR will be involved in crafting these key messages. However, what seems like a simple task—write an email about organizational changes for the leadership team to share with employees, and then send that email—turns out to be somewhat complicated.

Timing is critical with these messages. Keri often needed to coach leaders on why it is critical to share a message with a group of employees on a certain day and at a certain time—and not a minute later. How would you feel about receiving an email from the leadership team about layoffs in your department before even your own manager informed you? Poor communication plans can significantly damage employee morale. Careful management of communication plans helps ease the pain of difficult messages. As difficult as these messages may be for employees, Keri encouraged leaders to follow the communication plan to the letter so that they showed value and respect for everyone involved.

For example, with a communication plan detailing layoffs, Keri could have opted to draft an email, obtain required approval sign-offs, and let the executive team take the work from that point on. It takes courage to be the one in the room who says "Slow down. We need a thoughtful communication plan first." It also takes courage to say "We need to follow the communication plan timing precisely" or "We did not follow the cadence of communications, and we must course-correct immediately." HR Warriors need to be ready to have tough conversations, and most leaders will see the benefit of following their advice.

Not Everyone Will Love You

In the age of social media, it's easy to see who likes and who doesn't like what you say. With one click, you can "thumbs-up" or "heart" what others post. No hidden agenda. It's foolproof! In the workplace, we may not walk around and hand a red paper heart to those colleagues we enjoy working with. But in subtle ways, we do recognize if we've made an enemy.

HR is very familiar with the nuances of unfriendliness. Although some of the dislike is not personal (it's business), HR's bad rap has caused clients and business leaders to avoid us unless absolutely necessary. As Michael Scott said in a TV episode of *The Office*, "What's the only thing worse than one HR rep? Two HR reps."

We've discussed why HR has a bad reputation in some organizations—and that our goal with this book is to be accountable for what we can do to change our reality. Because HR Warriors can do a lot to change the negative perception.

No one likes administrative work (except maybe those irreplaceable executive assistants who have a special gift of maintaining order). HR has administrative tasks we must manage, such as annual compliance training, and we nag. Not because we want to, but because we must. Most importantly, we understand the bigger picture of why those tasks are crucial to the business.

Many parents have used the following line on their kids: "Punishing you hurts me more than it hurts you." Kids roll their eyes at this in disbelief. After all, how does their revoking your cell phone privileges hurt them?

When you're chasing down employees and managers who haven't completed their compliance training, you may feel like a parent chasing their children. But just like parents, HR Warriors do it for a greater cause: they care about the short- and long-term success of the business.

"You must complete the anti-harassment course by the end of the week!"

"Why?"

"Because it's a requirement."

"Why?"

"Because it's in the employee handbook."

"Why?"

"Because it is our company culture not to create negative and intimidating environments for our employees."

That's not a fun conversation. Well, to be honest, sometimes it *can* lead to fun. Have you ever felt so overwhelmed by your workload that it is actually fun to sort and stack envelopes in the breakroom? Taking a step away from emotionally charged jobs and completing a tactical task can serve as a Zen-like rebalancing of the crazy with the mundane.

HR Warriors accept that employees are not going to like receiving emails about incomplete compliance courses. But they send the emails anyway. HR Warriors understand that managers don't want to be bothered with a weekly check-in on who of their direct reports is out of compliance, but they book that meeting to review the report with them nonetheless. Why? Because HR Warriors care more about the organizational implications for noncompliance than whether people like them.

KERI'S TEAMS OFTEN PARTNER with Talent Acquisition (TA) on managing the hiring process. Although the TA team sources candidates, coordinates interviews, completes the background check, and relays details that come after an accepted offer, the HR team remains involved to ensure that the "candidate experience" was positive and that the hiring managers were happy about the efficiency of the process. This last one isn't always the case. No surprise. Sometimes the process doesn't work well because of the candidate's expectations or last-minute requests, or TA or HR didn't manage all details precisely. Sometimes it was a hiring manager who made an error, or a combination of all these variables (those are fun examples!).

Keri experienced an all-too-familiar scenario when a hiring manager moved too quickly: "I want to hire Jane, and I want her to start on Monday."

Keri received this news with concern—it was a decision that had skipped over about eight steps in the process and was missing a few emails.

Her first question began the same way: "Do you have a job description?" The blank stare of the hiring manager she got in response told her all she needed to know. The manager wanted to hire someone and figure out the details later. But those details were important—both legally and strategically. "We need a job description," Keri said, "and *before* we hire Jane."

When sharing bad news, Keri often feels like a parent telling a child to finish their homework before playing video games. But in this example, the consequences are far greater than turning in a science assignment late. Hiring an employee without following the proper steps placed the company in a risky situation, and Keri's job was to keep managers out of compliance jail.

But more than that, she needed to understand the rationale for the new hire's role. Did the branch need another employee right now? And was the expectation for this role clear, before the person is hired?

Sometimes the response from the manager to hurry through (and around) the hiring steps was dramatic, even if the concerns were legitimate: "I don't have one, and I don't have time to write one. I need Jane to start in three days. My branch is dying out there!"

Keri's response? "HR wants the right talent in the right roles. And we want to help you hire employees the right way. That being said, we can certainly move the process as quickly as possible for you." Compromise, Keri learned, was the fine line between following processes and serving business goals in the workplace.

COMPROMISE, ALONG WITH EDUCATION, helps managers understand HR's recommendations. Rather than dictating to the manager what they can and cannot do, it's best to explain the rationale for recommending certain steps. And then all can move mountains for them to achieve a common goal.

Warriors help their clients win, even if the client doesn't want the help. In the earlier example of going to the next level to provide thorough feedback on a sales candidate, it is clear that the HR partner has a say in the hiring process. But what if you do not recommend this candidate, whereas the rest of the hiring panel wants to draft the offer? You will learn quickly whose opinions rank supreme, and how difficult it can be to voice the unpopular opinion.

HR Warriors are willing to be unpopular because they have a different perspective on the company. They see how new hires will interact on a personal level with others, how their past perspectives and personality will mix with the existing culture, and what gaps exist within the team that the candidate can bridge.

Warriors have valuable insights and are not afraid to share their insights with others, even if those insights are contrary to popular opinion.

Go Toe to Toe

If you've ever watched a football game, you'll have noticed that every play starts with the opposing teams lined up facing each other along an invisible line—the line of scrimmage. The players are awfully close to each other—close enough to whisper taunts, jabs, and threats to their opponents. Eyes on eyes, helmets on helmets, knees on knees, separated by only inches and an invisible line. If anyone crosses this line early, a penalty is called.

Once the whistle blows, it's game on. Sometimes HR Warriors must put on their helmets and shoulder pads. Sometimes they must go to battle for their team, for their philosophy, for their environment. Sometimes Warriors must fight. Fighting for what's right in the workplace is courageous. As explained earlier, courage takes effort, and this is seen clearly in moments where we can go with the flow or be a salmon swimming against the current.

For instance, what do you do if the leader of the Finance Department allows one of his beleaguered managers take his frustrations out on lower-level employees?

You've participated in one-on-one conversations and feedback sessions, and given the manager invites to leadership development courses. But this manager does not want to change. He is not receptive—he is set in his ways. And why

Warriors are **not afraid to share their valuable insights,** even if those insights are contrary to popular opinion.

would he change, if he's been with the organization for fifteen years and continually earns a merit increase year after year? Put your helmet on, march onto the turf, and go toe to toe with leadership.

Although you probably don't want to be viewed as a whistleblower, at times it is necessary to escalate concerns up the chain of command. This is not a self-promoting exercise; this is being a steward of the company environment and the company culture.

Schedule that meeting with the head of Finance. Arrive prepared with your notes, highlights (and lowlights), and recommendations. What do you think could alleviate the pressure felt by this manager's behavior? What could improve the team environment? What will help this manager identify his errors and acknowledge the impact on his team? Bring the solutions, don't just identify the problems!

The head of the department may not want to hear what you must say. He may resist. He may deny reality. He may not have the stomach to make a tough decision—or worse, he may not care. That shouldn't negate your commitment to show courage and have that conversation anyway. But when you bring solutions to the meeting, demonstrating that you are placing yourself in the leader's shoes, you build trust. You build teamwork. HR and the business: in it together, and in it to win it!

Doing what's right takes courage, and sometimes doing what's right is to push back on leaders when they are not receptive to feedback. Push back with reasons, and follow up with solutions. Warriors demonstrate the ability to problem-solve together, rather than just cutting a hole in the existing plans to show how penetrable they are. And sometimes, we must have this same courage with HR partners.

WHEN MONICA LAUNCHED her HR career, she was fortunate to have several experienced HR leaders who she considered mentors. They taught her much of what she knows today, providing her with insights, strategies, and tips for success in just a few years. They taught her the basics when she knew nothing about Human Resources. (By the way, what is an FTE?)

One of the most invaluable lessons a mentor of hers taught her was how to speak up. Monica had good ideas and needed to share them. HR Warriors share thoughts with business partners, in part to build an honest and trusting relationship with them. But initially Monica was reluctant. Share her thoughts publicly? As in out loud? Yikes!

Her mentor noticed her hesitancy at speaking out at team meetings. But slowly and gradually, Monica began speaking up. She shared a few of her ideas and her team was receptive. "Okay, not so bad," Monica thought.

Later on, with a few years of experience under her belt— but still early in her career—Monica was part of an HR reorganization that shifted her role to one that supported a different division, with less responsibility. She had a new manager and a new job description she didn't like. She was less than excited about these changes in HR. In fact, she was angered by them. Monica had been delivering good work to her clients and was working towards a promotion. In her mind, she was twelve months from taking on an HR managerial position. All this changed with the reorganization.

Her new manager could sense her frustration. They had an initial one-on-one meeting to lay the ground rules for their working relationship, the cadence of communications, who would own what work with their client group, and how their roles differed in level of responsibilities. Monica had concerns after this meeting. She felt she could do more and that her development plan was offtrack. In a second meeting, she shared these concerns with her manager, who appeared to listen.

But nothing changed. After a few weeks, Monica decided to meet with her manager again—her concerns were being heard, but why was nothing happening? She expressed her desire to be challenged, to take on more work, to find a way to that promotion. Again, weeks went by and nothing changed.

What eventually became apparent were the larger circumstances at play. Monica's HR organization had made the reorganizational decisions for specific reasons—reasons she was not aware of. There was a fundamental shift taking place as to what the level of service HR would provide to the business, and this would have an impact on everyone. It can be difficult to see the forest for the trees, especially when you are wrapped up in your own job. When her manager shared these insights with her, Monica finally understood, though she told her manager that she disagreed with the direction the company was taking. And that's okay.

This exercise was practice in voicing her opinion, and also practice in taking an unpopular stance. She understood the importance of remaining respectful of leadership while giving transparent feedback. She felt concerned that her reaction would be interpreted as antagonistic and unnecessarily difficult, but she had learned to speak up anyway. By going toe to toe with her manager and sharing what was important to her for her career path, Monica exhibited a great deal of courage.

An HR Weenie may be tempted to take the easy way out, complaining to HR peers about the organization's changes rather than having a thorough discussion with a manager. Difficult conversations are a valuable part of a trustworthy working relationship.

NO MATTER THE TYPE of relationship, you will not always agree with others. It can take courage to be respectful of others' opinions and to share your own. Managing this balancing act effectively is what differentiates an HR Warrior from an HR Weenie.

Courage in the Workplace

Courage can be a tricky quality to incorporate in your quest to be an HR Warrior because it can be misunderstood. Do you appear combative, hostile, or unfriendly? Will making sure you are heard have a negative impact on your career opportunities? Will you get fired for speaking up? A fine balance does exist between showing courage and showing resistance.

When Warriors display courage, they:

- Strike a balance between acting with courage and embracing any fear they may have. They don't let fear stop them from acting.

- Share feedback even when they know it's not the popular opinion or it challenges the leadership opinion.

- Raise awareness with the leadership team when leadership seems unaware of concerns, negative feedback, or rumblings occurring among employees.

- Speak up immediately when there are legal implications of certain decisions. At a minimum, this is what HR is paid to do!

- Don't always give the quick-fix answer but, rather, express the best solution to every problem, no matter how long (or how much money) it will take.

- Represent the employee when sharing perspective, plans, and preferences for how the workplace operates.

- Don't change just because others don't like them. They do what is right, when it's right, for the right reasons, regardless of others' opinions.

- Don't seek out the approval of others but instead seek out the truth.

- Speak up, regardless of the position of the person they're addressing—that is, whether CEO or entry-level employee.

Sometimes an HR Warrior must pick the least sucky option. There are pros and cons to any difficult business decision, and sometimes even many cons; find the option with the fewest.

When Warriors lack courage they:

- Remain silent in the workplace because it will create a stir. It's far easier to adopt groupthink.

- Avoid taking on more work because they don't have the time (or desire).

- Avoid building partnership with leaders who don't like HR. "If they don't like me, I don't want to work with them."

- Keep a list of enemies and frenemies in a note on the desktop, with a reminder to stay away from these people.

- Ignore the concerns of employees on minor issues (my desk cube partner talks too loud on the phone), because it's an issue that will probably go away if ignored. Probably.

- Refuse to speak out against a leader's decision, thinking,

"They could influence my career, after all, so I need them to like me."

If we had to drill down to the core of courageous, it would look like this: working in HR is not a popularity contest but an opportunity to make the workplace a more successful, engaging, and mutually beneficial environment through our influence.

A Recap

We've covered a lot of ground in describing what it means to be courageous in our careers, our environments, and our workplace. Let's now recap the multiple ways in which HR Warriors demonstrate courage:

- They do not take the easy way out. Accomplishing significant changes, and having significant influence in their workplace, means working hard. Sometimes you must work hard to see the smallest changes. Get after it.

- They are not everyone's best friend. They may show up on a naughty list here and there, but that doesn't stop them. They do not seek the approval of others, but instead seek to make the right decision regardless of approval. You don't need the title of "workplace BFF"!

- They go toe to toe with leadership. Unfortunately but not surprisingly, leaders don't always make the right decisions. HR has a voice that should be used to speak up when necessary.

Using our influence, working in HR is an opportunity to make the workplace **more successful, engaging, and mutually beneficial for all employees.**

The Check-In

This is an opportunity to check in on your current situation by considering questions about your commitment to courage in the workplace and in your career:

- Have you ever had the opportunity to take the easy way out and chose to do so? How did you feel about that decision?

- When did you put in the extra effort? Can you recall the impact of making that choice?

- What are three activities you have the opportunity in your current role to do that are not required of you but would make an impact on others?

- Do you know of someone in the workplace who doesn't like you? (No names please!) Can you pinpoint the reason for this, and if so, do you have the courage to address it with this person?

- What is your next opportunity to sit down with a manager or leader? Will you have the courage to use this opportunity to share feedback you have neglected to share about an unpopular opinion or decision?

Courage isn't about numbers or charts or an HR textbook on the basics of employment law. Courage is a heart issue and, as you will discover, the HR Warrior is a mix of heart and head. Some days are more heart than head, and some days are more head than heart. In the following chapters, you will learn how to strike the balance between the two and be the Warrior your company needs.

C**H**ARGE

CHAPTER 4

H Is for Humility

SOON AFTER INTERVIEWING a candidate, Keri received a thank-you card from him in the mail. How thoughtful! Hold that thought.

The candidate didn't compliment the company or the way the hiring process was handled, nor thank her for the opportunity, but instead called out her huge smile during their hour together. Given the context of their meeting, this was an unusual response. After years of interviewing candidates, Keri has developed a keen sense of nonverbal cues that weigh into her overall impression. Body language, eye contact, the handshake—all these provide insight into the candidate's personality and demeanor.

And what she had noticed is that this candidate had awkward nonverbal cues. Verbally he was impressive. His command of the subject matter, his responses to her open-ended questions, his explanation of prior roles and transitions as he described his résumé—all were presented effectively. But the nonverbal cues, followed by the handwritten thank-you note, were not appropriate.

Keri shared this feedback with the hiring team. They brushed it off as a faulty gut check, but she disagreed. In her expert opinion, this was not the right candidate for this job. The candidate was hired anyway, and within six months, Keri's team was coaching the department leader on performance concerns and the workplace behavior of this new hire. The next time Keri met with that leader, he mentioned this "problem child."

"He was a bad hire, and you told us so." The employee had been fired for inappropriate behavior and his departure had a serious impact on the team.

Keri paused. "We've all done it. I have made bad hiring decisions too, but we learn from it and move on."

The two continued with the meeting's agenda, never mentioning the situation again.

THERE MAY BE TIMES when an HR Warrior will need to swallow the words lest they come out of their mouth: "I was right and you were wrong." It takes humility to not announce your smarts to the world. But it's more productive to express humility through the work you do every day.

Each of the Warrior qualities discussed in this book is part of a strong foundation. Some of this information may seem basic, and quite honestly, that is the point. The foundation for an HR Warrior is basic, but it *is* a requirement. It's the flour in a bread recipe. It's the treadmill in the workout. It's the gasoline in the car. You get the point.

A foundational quality for an HR Warrior is to be humble. Although this may seem self-explanatory, humility is expressed in many ways. The list below describes ways in which humility shows up in the daily work of an HR Warrior.

As an HR Warrior, you—

- Ask questions. This happens naturally when you surround yourself with smart people, are open to feedback, and want to experience career opportunities in an unconventional manner. Ask three people for their advice before making a decision—getting the viewpoint of others can be very insightful!

- Accept that leaders make the business decisions—you do not. Even if they make decisions with which you disagree, you still support them, as the goal is the same: organizational (and consequently, employee) success.

- Act honorably, aware that everyone is watching you. HR has a unique position through which to represent the moral compass of the company, and the HR Warrior cannot take shortcuts when it comes to ethics, honesty, and honor. HR Warriors are values-driven employees.

- Admit to your mistakes quickly. When a mistake is made, humility enables you to accept that you will make mistakes but can recover from them and move on.

You as the reader may be thinking, "Isn't someone just either humble or not humble?" Well, yes, and no. Some people have powerful ego drives. (Think of the professional athlete who refers to himself in the third person, or the ex who didn't understand what "compromise" meant.) We all know at least one person like this. On the other hand, some people naturally gravitate towards a lifestyle of humility. (Think of the neighbor who spends every weekend volunteering for community groups without broadcasting this at the annual block party, or the best friend who has never shared the fact that she's a published songwriter.)

And then there is self-taught humility, when you are forced into a position of humility directly after an embarrassing mishap, a "teaching moment," or a flat-out you-are-100-percent-wrong moment. Ah, those are fun moments. As in Keri's story at the start of this chapter, humility can be learned through experience. "I told you so" doesn't get us very far in life. But "I've been there, so I understand" does.

Our hope is that you will choose humility, rather than humility choosing you. In your career, you will need to make a conscious effort to choose humility. But why is humility so essential? Because without it, you are not likely to admit when

You will need to make a conscious effort to **choose humility in your HR career.**

you need to change. And the easiest way to discover that you need to change is to surround yourself with smart people.

HR Weenies are far more likely to avoid smart people. Why? They do not want to be challenged. They want to have the appearance of intellectual superiority.

Ask Questions

An old saying that's been repeated many times, and in various ways, goes something like this: "Never be the smartest person in the room." Surround yourself by those who can teach you something. Seek out coworkers and managers from whom you can learn. Here are a few ideas:

- Attend optional meetings in which managers, other department leaders, or industry experts will be speaking.

- Join luncheons, conferences, and events that stretch you mentally. It doesn't have to be a high-cost event; low-cost events present great opportunities to network and connect with insightful people also.

- Schedule "skip level" meetings. This is a meeting with your manager's manager. Have a list of questions prepared, and ask away!

- Attend those company-wide meetings that are not mandatory. Take notes. Be brave enough to ask a question.

- Listen to podcasts while you drive or are on public transit. Business-related, education-related, and knowledge-based podcasts can offer you an "automobile university" education, whether you are sitting in your car or on the train or bus during your daily commute.

- Read books (besides this one). You can start by checking out the ones we list in the Select Resources section (page 201).

- Get mentored by the most successful and brilliant minds in our world without ever meeting them in person. Many of them speak on TV, talk on podcasts, and write books. Chase them down! We guarantee that they have something valuable to say that you really should listen to. Let them be the smart ones in the conversation.

If you adopt several of the suggestions listed above, you will be in the minority. You will be someone who takes their humility seriously and receives a great reward for listening to intelligent and insightful people. Even the greatest influencers of our time have mentors who played a role in their growth and success.

But be prepared for what happens when you listen to smart people: you realize you've got a long way to go. Now, that's humbling.

Have you ever tried to follow a recipe for a complicated dish? If you are someone whose definition of cooking is boiling water, you will feel overwhelmed when you are asked to make beef Wellington for Sunday family dinner. Those chefs on the Food Network make it look so easy! They have years (and years) of practice. They've made plenty of mistakes, started a kitchen fire or two, and quite possibly served meals where the diner's face scrunches up in disgust and the food is spat into a napkin. In those moments of serving truly horrendous meals, the chefs realize they have a long way to go before their cooking skills are camera-ready.

You can experience the same humility in the workplace. When you surround yourself with smart people, you will inevitably participate in conversations that are over your head.

You may ask questions for which the answers only serve to confuse you further. You may even present a solution to a complex workplace conflict, only to have it fall flat. Take a deep breath. Be thankful for the opportunity to be humbled.

Understand this: during every opportunity you take to communicate, partner, and work with inventive and creative people, you are developing your humility muscle. The larger this muscle grows, the more you look and act like an HR Warrior.

Business Leaders Make Business Decisions

Leaders make the business decisions, and it's HR's function to support these decisions—even when they disagree with them. This does not mean acting in an unethical way or turning your back on misbehavior in the workplace. And it doesn't mean staying silent when you disagree. What it does mean is calling upon your humility to focus on common goals: the business goals.

We discuss later the importance of understanding your organization's business goals (see Chapter 7)—it is one indispensable way that Warriors can create influence in the workplace. But since humility is the topic here . . . why would focusing on your company's goals be humbling? Because it's not about you. It's about the employees and clients you work with. There is no "I" in Warri—hold on. There is no "I" in "Human Resources"!

Do you remember learning to drive, with one of your parents as the passenger? They pressed the invisible brake below the glove box with their foot. They began shouting when you were still two blocks away from the yellow light. They told you to check your mirror positions—again and again. It was annoying, wasn't it? You knew what to do. You just needed to be trusted. Our business leaders feel the same way. The size of their paychecks is directly proportional to the trust placed in them to make big business decisions. The bigger the paycheck, the bigger the decisions.

Warriors understand that we do not make the business decisions. Say what? You read that right. When it comes to launching a new product line, opening another store, implementing an international marketing plan, selling to a new client, creating a new division, closing a business unit, or even hiring a new CEO—Human Resources does not get the final say.

The HR Warrior is more than a "seat at the table." Warriors move from office to office, from conversation to conversation, intimately aware of the goals of the business and how they can be achieved, before the boardroom meetings take place. And when the boardroom meetings take place and the big decisions are made, you may not always agree with the outcome. Warriors find a way to work towards the organization's goals despite these challenges.

"WHAT SHOULD I do now?"

Managers ask this of HR for many reasons, and usually after an unwelcome surprise in the workplace. Keri's colleague, let's call her Amber, had to quickly deal with an unpredictable situation when a manager showed up drunk to lead a training class.

Amber has led many training classes over the course of her career. She had worked as a performance consultant for numerous companies, and managers who partnered with her to lead training classes had acted as true professionals. Usually.

This manager showed up drunk and disheveled, smelling of alcohol and fumbling his words. Amber, who had organized the training class, announced to participants that the session would start within thirty minutes but would not be led by that manager. She acted immediately. She adjusted the speaker's schedule and notified her HR partner and the leadership team.

Amber expected that this would be the last time she would see this manager. But this wasn't the case. Instead, although the leadership team listened to HR's feedback, they did not feel his behavior warranted termination or even a warning. In fact, they wanted HR to "stand down."

Stand down? Amber couldn't believe this response, and she couldn't disagree with it more. Amber shared the story with Keri (venting made up a significant portion of the conversation—Amber was in shock!). Keri and Amber swapped stories of other such workplace disasters, enjoying a few laughs, but ultimately concluded that Warriors don't make the business decisions. We find a way to work with our leaders and fight for the best outcome possible.

And the best outcome (other than the class going off without a hitch) did occur: the training was a huge success. And the employees did not start their morning exposed to a drunken manager.

IN THE EXAMPLE ABOVE, Amber had to make a difficult decision, but she accepted the business leaders' decision, even if their values did not align with her own. At times, the decisions that leaders make are outside the boundaries of the acceptable. They may cross a moral or values-driven line. When this occurs, another level of courage will be required of you. But how does a Warrior respond when a leader makes a decision they do not agree with yet does not cross that values-driven line? They use their influence to improve employee experience.

Perhaps the decision to close a business unit has an immediate and painful impact on the employee base. Human Resources can manage the communication process: When will the employees be told? What will the message be? What can we provide the affected employees to ease the pain? Do we have any open positions in other business units, to save jobs?

Or, although you may not agree with the decision to outsource a portion of the Technology Department, what can you as an HR Warrior do in response? You can offer outplacement services to help displaced employees update their résumés. Provide recruiting services to help employees find their next role. And set up one-on-one appointments to listen to the employees, even if all you can do is just that—listen.

Values First

Disagreements in the workplace do not stop HR Warriors. Humility is perhaps the foundational quality needed most in those times of disagreement. Act honorably by respecting the roles we play, and the roles we do not play. And one inherited HR role is representing the moral compass of the company.

This is not to say HR always acts perfectly. Anyone can do a quick internet search to find stories of bad behavior in the workplace that HR leaders have ignored—behavior we will not mention here! (And no need to email us and share what you found—been there, done that, seen that. Unless it's an amazingly outrageous story...) Humility requires that a Warrior act honorably, even if no one is conducting an internet search on our company. We are in a unique place to set the moral standard, and this means we don't take shortcuts. We cannot ignore the advice we dish out. We Warriors practice what we preach. We lead the CHARGE!

Imagine you are like a goldfish. Even if the goldfish works hard at hiding behind fake sandcastles, weeds, and coral, you can still see its every move. And although no one likes to think of themselves as working in a fishbowl, there's no denying that HR is being watched. Employees want to see if HR will hold themselves to the same rules and standards as they hold others to.

When HR asks employees to complete the annual compliance courses by a certain due date, is HR itself the first department to reach 100 percent completion? When they ask managers to document performance concerns about their direct reports, does HR hold themselves accountable for doing the same? If HR asks leaders to complete each step in the new-hire onboarding plan, do they have the same standard for themselves?

Warriors demonstrate humility by **asking others to do what they themselves demonstrate first.**

Unfortunately for HR, too many Weenies will hold a separate standard for their business partners. "Do as I say, not as I do" is their motto.

It is difficult to take seriously someone who cannot be trusted. Warriors demonstrate humility by asking others to do what they themselves demonstrate first. And that is how an HR Warrior becomes a values-first employee. Warriors are not bottom line first, or reputation first, or even HR first. They are values first. And when daily actions are led by strong values, they become bottom line, reputation positive.

What does it look like to be values first? You—

- Show respect for scheduled meetings. Show up on time, wrap up on time. Value the time of others.

- Respond to emails within twenty-four hours. Even if you don't have the answer to the question, you acknowledge the email: "I don't have the answer yet, but I will get back to you tomorrow." Value the questions of others.

- Listen well. When you have difficult, one-on-one conversations with employees, reserve a secluded conference room with no windows, and bring tissues and a notebook to record key takeaways. Sit patiently and silently, let the employee speak, and express value for their concerns.

- Go the extra mile to help employees go that extra mile too. Many employees have their own goals—they want to earn more money or a promotion, be recognized for the great work they do. Fight for them! Help build development plans; remain attentive to job openings and refer employees to them; spend time in private conversations, encouraging employees to take on stretch assignments within their functions. HR Warriors value the opportunities of employees.

AFTER SPENDING FIVE YEARS as an HR generalist, Monica had the opportunity to learn more about recruiting by taking on a role in Talent Acquisition. This was a challenging transition for her.

When she stepped into this role, Monica had no preconceptions of how the day-to-day work occurred. She didn't have the experience or education of other recruiters, which gave her a different take on how to operate. The metric-driven, commission-based role meant she needed to adjust her priorities. It presented challenges similar to the role of Sales, and with this change came a competitive edge.

One of the first positions Monica recruited for was a sales executive in the mid-Atlantic market. She used her tools to search for qualified candidates and began scheduling conversations with interested people. This client had numerous roles available in other markets in the country, and these were open roles her recruiting partners were focused on.

Monica had candidates nationwide apply for the sales executive position, and she had several strong candidates to offer. But since the client was not willing to relocate a candidate, her candidates weren't a fit for the sales position. But they were a fit for the other open positions elsewhere. She shared their names, résumés, and contact information with one of her recruiting partners. The client benefited from interviewing these candidates, and Monica and her partner benefited from showcasing the level of talent they could deliver.

Monica sent the information through the team's applicant tracking system (ATS) and continued her local search. But she soon discovered how unusual her information-sharing was when one of her recruiting partners called to say "You're willing to share candidates. You are not like other recruiters I've worked with!" That was surprising to Monica: Why *wouldn't* she want to share candidates with her teammates?

Not long after, she received similar feedback from a coworker who had an open position in Texas. Monica had spoken with a candidate looking for a job in that market, and since the candidate was more than qualified for the role, Monica submitted her details to her coworker. But this time, Monica picked up the phone beforehand to talk to her coworker and explain the situation.

"If this candidate is placed in this role," Monica said, "you can have a role I'm working on. I know that technically I found the candidate, so I will get the commission, but then it will balance out because you take on one of my open roles." What Monica didn't realize is that many recruiting firms do not work this way. Because of the way "candidate ownership" is structured, many recruiters tend to keep their arms around good talent they find, thinking that perhaps in the future they will find a role for that person.

Recruiting talent is commission-driven work, and Monica understood this, but she also knew she wanted her company and her recruiting partners to succeed. She believed "If I win, everyone wins."

WHEN WE PRACTICE humility in the workplace, we become values-driven, and that approach is cross-functional. Those values will carry us through every job and career change we make.

Confession Is Good for the HR Soul

Another aspect of humility is admitting when you are wrong. People make mistakes all day long—whether in our personal lives or our professional lives, mistakes are inevitable. The key is to turn a negative into a positive. Own it. Learn from it. And move on (as a slightly better version of yourself).

You may have overpromised and underdelivered to one of your clients. You may have missed a deadline, didn't meet expectations, didn't follow through. Okay—say it. It's a great sign of maturity (and a great way to build trust) when you can admit to a business partner, a client, a manager, or a coworker that you made a mistake. And the important thing is to admit it. Not to yourself, or to your cat or dog at home, but to the person who also knows you made the mistake.

KERI AND HER TEAM led a large change management project that was responsible for many lessons in humility. And one lesson was very humbling for Monica, one of the team members. She was responsible for tracking the new payroll budget for an East Coast region as they moved current employees into new roles. The new roles, coming out of the organization's realignment, meant some employees would be getting a slight pay increase, some would be getting a slight decrease, and many would be maintaining their current salary.

The team monitored every dollar for a forty-eight-hour period. The general manager had a specific salary cap, and the spreadsheet Monica had in front of her listed every employee name, every job title, and the maximum salary for each. She checked it once, twice, three times.

But still Monica messed up. After she had submitted the final, GM-approved spreadsheet to the Finance Department,

Finance sent her an email: "We've found discrepancies in your report." The GM was over budget by several thousand dollars. In other words, in the world of finance, she wasn't even close in her tracking.

Monica had a knot in her stomach when she read the email, but she knew she had to share this news with the GM. She knew her boss would be angry. She was angry with herself. She gave him the update, and she was right—he was furious. The silver lining, however, was that the team was able to resubmit the salary spreadsheet before any employees were given the wrong salary.

THE SOONER WE CONFESS to making a mistake, the less damage that is done. It's easy to hide and save face when we make mistakes, but we do more damage to others when we try to preserve ourselves.

Own it. Eat that slice of humble pie.

Speed is key in recovering from a mistake. Maybe you should have given yourself more time to complete the project. Maybe you should have stayed at work ten minutes longer to read and respond to those three emails. Your favorite TV show is streaming on demand anyway, so you really didn't have to rush home to watch it.

If it's an easy fix, do it! If it's a hard fix—let's say you have a reputation for being late for meetings and now your business partners pushed you off the agenda—do it as well! Some fixes are quick, others take time. Character can be ruined in a day, and it takes a long time to rebuild.

Humility in the Workplace

Warriors can, with daily diligence, develop humility—just like any muscle. Although its growth may be small and incremental, humility is essential for becoming an HR Warrior. So be sure these key components make it into your daily routine in the workplace:

- If your client disagrees with your recommendations, respect their point of view. Present data to support your decisions, but know when to relent.

- If you are going to fight, know why, and support it with concrete evidence. Assemble all the facts and as much data as you can gather. Business leaders value data.

- Present your argument with the utmost respect and professionalism. How we say something is sometimes just as valuable as what we say.

- Accept defeat gracefully.

- Upon accepting defeat, do not badmouth leaders, gossip in the hallways at work, or continually bring up the issue. Let it go.

- Fight the urge to say "I told you so."

- Champion the business cause and look to win the next day!

- Admit when you are wrong.

- Learn from your mistakes. If you are wrong, find out why. Dig in and explore the reasons, adjusting so that you don't repeat past mistakes.

That's a straightforward process for how to handle many workplace divides. But just as important is knowing how *not* to handle them. Here are behaviors to avoid if you want to be an HR Warrior:

- Clinging on to an opinion despite few supporting facts.

- Avoiding the truth out of fear you could be proven wrong.

- Telling off a leader.

- Remaining silent when you are wrong.

- Not setting an example for proper behavior in a professional environment.

A Recap

Sometimes it's painful to act like a humble Warrior, but when you keep your eyes on the company "prize," it's worth it. Remember:

- Ask questions. Don't be shy or feel ashamed if you don't know something (no matter how basic). Stretch yourself and learn from people far smarter than you.

- Respect that the leaders are paid to make the tough decisions. Although HR brings a unique perspective to any complex scenario, you don't make the business decisions. Humility means finding ways to support leadership regardless of the outcome, because we want to continue accomplishing the larger business goals within the workplace environment.

- Act with honor. You are being watched! Whether the business leaders like us or not, they do watch how we behave. Humility equals credibility. Walk first and talk second. Set examples, and hold others accountable to the same.

- Admit your mistakes. HR doesn't have all the answers, nor does any other function. Course-correct quickly and efficiently to minimize damage created by your mistake, because you've got work to do!

The Check-In

Developing your humility muscle allows you to maximize your strengths and flex your brainpower. But you also need to be humble about the work you do, and the solutions you present. Check in with your own sense of humility by asking yourself:

- When was the last time you admitted (out loud) that you were wrong?

- When was the last time you fought the urge to say "I told you so"?

- Can you identify someone you've worked with who exemplified the quality of humility in a great way? How so?

- Can you think of a workplace scenario in which HR and the business were on completely different sides of the spectrum? Whose opinion held firm, and whose needed to bend?

- If you were the HR leader in that scenario, knowing what you know now about the importance of humility, how would you handle that situation?

CH<u>A</u>RGE

CHAPTER 5
A Is for Accuracy

LAYOFFS ARE AN UNFORGETTABLE experience for most employees. Ask anyone about their work history during an interview and their face will twitch as they admit that they have been laid off by an employer. HR is at the forefront of planning and executing these layoffs, and Monica has certainly been involved in these contentious events, sometimes in a condensed time frame.

One specific layoff stands out more than any other for Monica, mostly because of how a seemingly impersonal situation became personal. Word came from a director that a small team of front-line employees would be laid off because of low production. This layoff would occur, unfortunately, in December and could not wait until January. After a quick assessment, a handful of employees were selected to be let go. Monica sat in on each of the conversations with the affected employee and their manager. The employees' reactions were all different—ranging from anger to silence to tears. But what Monica learned after that full day of these conversations provided her with an opportunity to make a situation better. And to make someone much happier.

Sometimes it seems that certain departments in large companies work in isolation. What happens in one area seemingly functions independently from another, and this can result in a lack of communication between teams. In her role as a generalist, Monica helped not only with hiring, onboarding, and promotions but also with performance plans, terminations, and layoffs—the full employee life cycle. When the aforementioned layoffs occurred, Monica quickly realized that another department held the solution.

While one department was laying off employees, another was hiring. Why were the dots not connected prior to those difficult conversations with the employees? Unfortunately, the process had been rushed: the decision to lay off employees occurred only days before they were notified, so the door of opportunity to assess other options was never opened.

Monica reached out to the hiring department's leader— What positions are you hiring for? What are the required qualifications for those open roles? Turned out that the open positions required the employee to be forklift certified. And the manager from the department laying off employees did not specifically hire people who were forklift certified, as it was not required to do their jobs. Monica checked the files of all the laid-off employees and discovered that one had achieved this certification on his own, and had even picked up additional work hours driving a forklift in the department that was hiring. A few calls were made, and a new position (with a higher hourly wage) was offered to the employee.

Although this solution obviously was not a fix for everyone who was laid off, it did help one employee and his family.

HELPING ONE EMPLOYEE is sometimes all you can do in HR, but that is just as important as any other work you accomplish. When you operate with accuracy and find a specific solution that may help only one person, you can slowly change the landscape and, eventually, have an impact on many lives.

What do we mean by "operate with accuracy"? Accuracy is finding the root cause of any issue—whether it's a fledgling partnership, poor performance, or financial struggles. Honing your ability to be accurate in your work can make a big difference in your success as an HR Warrior. Here's what to do to achieve a high level of accuracy:

- Identify the pain points of any situation and, like a surgeon, remove them. You have been hired to identify the cause of the issue and come up with a lasting solution. This process is called a "root cause analysis."

- Be curious. Often the truth of any issue is buried far below the surface problem, and good surgeons prefer to find the root of the problem, rather than only alleviate the symptoms.

- Build trust with employees. HR Warriors make a personal connection with employees and deal with very real emotions—good and bad. Employees share their vulnerabilities with us in the hope that we can help alleviate the pain. Treat this bond with respect.

- Remain precise in the face of troubling times. Your days in the workplace may be unpredictable, but don't let that rock you.

- Take the time required to find the right solution (not just the easy or the quick solution).

- Respect and understand your work boundaries. Acknowledge existing boundaries (employment law, company procedures, department objectives, and individual roles) while you are problem-solving to come up with creative and effective solutions. You can't break the law, but you can be creative!

The Root Cause Analysis

Warriors demonstrate accuracy in their daily work. Accuracy means to identify the root cause of any issue. Indeed, it's the job of the HR Warrior to find the root cause of an issue, and this is usually accomplished through a root cause analysis.

So, what exactly is a root cause analysis?

A root cause analysis is similar to what a surgeon does in preparation for a surgery. You carefully identify the problem and determine the best solution. No, you won't need scalpels, and you won't need to scrub your arms before entering your workplace. And no one should run scared for fear of losing appendages. A root cause analysis can happen every day in the office when a problem arises. It involves asking: What is the pain, and what's really causing that pain?

In the business world, employees feel pain, leadership feels pain, and clients can feel pain. And the short-term high of a large paycheck or an invoice paid subsides rather quickly— these painkillers only work for so long. The best course of action for any organization is to get to the root cause of the pain—and eliminate it. And that requires strategic effort and accuracy.

How can you create a root cause analysis? Here's an example of how it works:

HR receives a lot of requests for team building and increasing team performance or morale. Problems exist, things aren't going well, business is not strong. Keri has heard this request often: "We need to bring the team together now and fix it."

But do they? Keri prefers to get to the root cause of the problems. Rather than immediately agreeing to spend time and money for an in-person meeting, her first step is accurately diagnosing the root problem affecting the team. Sometimes the diagnosis is surprising.

Dig into the team's culture. Interview employees. Interview leaders who work with the team. Ask a lot of questions, clarify what the team's expectations are, analyze the gap in perception. Keri implemented this process when she received a request for "team building." What she discovered was that the issue had nothing to do with what the manager assumed was the problem—the issue was one employee, critical to the success of the team, who had created a toxic environment with his behavior.

Keri recommended placing this employee on a performance plan instead of designing a team-building meeting for the entire team. Hers was an accurate response because it pinpointed the specific problem with the team's issues.

A root cause analysis takes time and effort. However, keep in mind that a root cause analysis is not a one-time solution. It is one tool that Warriors can use, just as a surgeon uses a scalpel, among other instruments.

Be Curious

The workplace can feel like a schoolyard at times:

- Ethan was rude to Sharie, and now Sharie doesn't want to partner with him on the Six Sigma project any longer.

- Tori feels her manager is micro-managing her because he requested a daily report of how she spends her time.

- John is a first-time CEO and has missed his quarterly numbers twice, yet he is taking much of his allotted vacation time.

- A phone call from someone claiming to be a company client alleges an inappropriate relationship between the procurement manager and the sales executive.

- Dari received a verbal warning for poor performance, but as the most tenured employee in her department, she reads this as age discrimination.

Sometimes the workplace feels like an afternoon soap opera, and when it does, curiosity is the most useful tool for getting to the bottom of the drama.

The first responsibility of an HR professional is to listen. But after listening, providing a temporary fix is not the answer. The goal should be to understand every aspect of the problem, including who is involved, and what was said and done, and to collect dates, details, and descriptions of all parties. Listening is a powerful action step; patients appreciate doctors who take the time to listen fully to their concerns.

Ask questions. *A lot* of questions. Ask about what happened prior to the conflict, during, and after. Ask what is going on within the team, and within the department. Ask what's going well. Ask why things seem to not be going well. Use your strong sense of curiosity to gather as much information as possible about a situation. These questions will help you gain clarity and become more accurate.

Rather than assume you understand the extent of the pain from having listened to the opening statement, dig deeper. Ask why, and ask why multiple times. Use the journalistic standard of "who, what, when, where, why, and how" to get the full story. Then repeat with each person involved. We need all the accurate information if we are going to identify the right solution.

EMPLOYEE INVESTIGATIONS ARE a key component in the job of an HR generalist. Monica was part of one investigation that was nothing short of a full-time job. She supported a team of fifty employees, a mix of full-time, part-time, contract, and work-from-home employees. The complication of these workplaces alone was challenging for the manager to track.

And that caused problems. Some employees felt underappreciated and overworked. Some employees resented clocking in at exactly 8 a.m. while coworkers rolled in at half past the hour. Some employees requested the privilege of working remotely, but only a few of these requests were granted. Employees began to grumble among themselves, complain to management, and eventually some delivered formal accusations of a discriminatory workplace.

Monica realized that the only way to understand the accusations was to speak with all the employees who had concerns and were willing to talk to HR about them. Her first conversations were with the three managers of the team, and then she spoke with almost twenty employees. All within a five-day period.

Why did she move on this so quickly? Because allegations of discrimination cannot go for long without a response. Any delay in responding would make it look like the company didn't care, even though this was not the case. So all other work was pushed to the side—in HR, schedules must be flexible! This investigation took priority—and a significant amount of documentation.

Monica had initial conversations, then second conversations, and then a third round of conversations with a select group of key employees. Statements didn't always align, new facts came to light, and further accusations were made. The situation was a tangled mess, and the concerns of the team were extensive and far-reaching. Although it took the investigation five days to identify the root cause of the frustrations, those five days revealed to the leadership team that the issues of this particular team had significant implications for the success of the company. The action plan was taken seriously and put into effect immediately.

Monica had the opportunity to represent the company in an emotionally charged situation. This was a long investigation and the stakes were high. The goal of the company was to avoid a lawsuit. The goal of the employee base was to receive concessions from management and create a better working environment. By meticulously unearthing the cause of the pain felt by the aggrieved employees, verifying the details shared by them, and diligently documenting everything, Monica identified the root cause of the problems. The healing process was long—because of the severity of the problems—but the company avoided a lawsuit and the concerned employees saw several substantial changes to their work environment.

Not everything was fixed after that first week, however. The changes within the department took six months to implement, which meant six months of additional conversations, follow-ups, action plans, adjustments, and policy revisions. This investigation became an important course-correct for a struggling department, but identifying the real pain points made the changes permanent.

Building Trust

Sometimes accuracy takes a lot of effort, and trust can make the difference between success and failure.

Many companies provide their employees with a survey that asks them various questions about their jobs, the company, and how they feel about the work they do. The survey results are then tallied to create a company "engagement score." At one of her prior companies, Keri supported a business unit that had some of the lowest employee engagement scores overall in the company, and the country leader wanted to know why. Anytime you have the eye and ear of the country leader, you know it's serious.

Keri and her HR team reviewed employee survey results region by region, and if any region had an engagement score of less than 50 percent, the regional leader worked with their HR partner to identify the reasons for the low score. Common issues were identified and then tied to specific action items meant to address the issues. Why were employees disengaged in their work, and what could be done to fix this? These action items required accountability from the leaders and from HR.

The regional leader, and the country leader, wanted the low engagement scores to improve. This is why it was so crucial to dig into the individual employee responses, even if this approach would take a significant amount of effort. Keri knew that what the employees wrote in their surveys would highlight sensitive and painful issues for the company, but identifying the pain points would yield high rewards.

By listening to employees, you demonstrate respect for their concerns and **a willingness to resolve the issue.**

Some managers, however, do not want to address the low engagement scores of their teams. Many reasons were behind their belief that scrutinizing the scores would not do any good: it took too long to assess their employees' answers, the results didn't carry much weight when it came to the business plans, and the scores were historically low (and likely would not change, regardless of any effort by the leadership team). But those same managers didn't reap the benefits of the surgical approach to removing the pain. Those managers who did create action plans using the employee feedback could concretely track activities that fixed problems and led to an improvement in engagement scores on the next employee survey.

TRUTH BE TOLD, we cannot force leaders to do what we want them to do. We can only demonstrate what happens when they do partner with us. We can be held accountable only if we agree on a plan together.

By listening to our employees, we demonstrate respect for their concerns and a willingness to resolve the issue. This is how we build trust, and this is how we can create plans to remove the pain. One conversation at a time.

Warriors create and maintain a high level of trust with employees and clients. You will often talk to employees in difficult and emotional situations, but Warriors find a way to remain strong in the face of them. We discuss this later but, for now, understand that the HR Warrior creates personal connections with employees through every interaction you have. You want employees to trust you enough to be vulnerable, in the hope that you can help alleviate their pain.

How does a Warrior know she's built trust with her employees?

- A manager calls her first when he gets bad news.

- A manager calls her first when he gets great news.

- Employees reach out to her when they want to vent, speak up, share concerns, or just have someone listen to them.

- She is invited to team meetings, and not just to be the note-taker but as an active participant, and placed on the agenda.

- She is asked for her opinions.

- She is recommended from one manager to the next, or from one client to the next.

- Her business partners are comfortable with providing her with feedback on her performance—good and bad.

Treat this bond with respect. It's a rarity to see in the workplace, but Warriors have it. Be proud of it when you do!

There Is No Magic Pill

An inside HR joke is that training is the cure, aka the "magic pill." Often, to solve a problem or issue within a team, managers will request that HR put together a training class and—*poof!*—the issue will disappear. Just like swallowing that magic pill. But a training class is not always the solution. It is important to first find out what the real issues are and to then determine whether a training program could fix them.

Problems that exist within a team, problems with an individual's performance, or problems with a business unit achieving its goals are rarely a training issue. Training can serve as a supplement to other solutions, but it is not the surgery itself. Often the root cause analysis reveals a struggle between employees and their manager, an issue with the ability of the manager to lead, or a lack of clarity about an individual's or the team's goals.

KERI REGULARLY RECEIVES phone calls from business partners asking for her help: employees on this team are not working well together; employees on that team have recorded historically low engagement scores; too many of the department's employees are underperforming and missing the mark on their key performance indicators (KPI). So, in a nutshell, the business is not doing well and needs Keri's help.

The HR Warrior creates personal connections with employees **through every interaction.**

Keri's response is always the same: "Let's do it!" Yet what she says next would seem to contradict: "Let's take the time to get to the root of the issue before preparing a solution." Some managers like her initial response, but not her next statement.

The first step in Keri's root cause analysis is to speak directly with employees. She schedules one-on-one conversations and asks the difficult questions. She places value on hearing firsthand what is happening on the team. What is going on day to day, what is said, what is felt, what are the priorities, what are the actions, and what are the results. This requires asking many open-ended questions and requires a lot of note-taking.

Keri also administers psychometric assessments, which is a fancy way of saying that she gives employees an assessment that digs into their personalities by asking questions. Under-standing an employee's personality helps Keri view the team environment through their eyes.

After having these individual conversations and perform-ing the assessments, Keri collects the responses in a formal feedback form for the manager, providing them with a lot of useful data. Typically, in Keri's experience, training is not the solution to the problems. Simply understanding the culture of the team, the personality dynamics, and the environmental influences will frequently allow the manager to devise cre-ative solutions without resorting to the "magic pill" of training.

Still, solving problems takes a significant amount of effort—which some managers don't want to hear. When Keri meets this kind of managerial resistance, she takes her approach a step further and helps the manager understand why it's better for the long-term health and benefit of the team to come up with a solution outside of training. Working with a manager to help them understand the root cause of an issue and creating a strategic plan to address it can be challenging. The manager wants a magic pill! These HR situations are often messy and emotional, but being accurate and diagnosing carefully is criti-cal to devising sustainable solutions.

Unpredictability Is the Norm

As much as some employees feel that their jobs are boring (and we all know someone who dreads Sunday nights because of the week-long slog ahead of them), HR is anything but. Busi-nesses would cease to exist if it weren't for people carrying out the work. But people are unpredictable. And that makes HR work unpredictable. Warriors don't let that rock them; they remain steady, precise, and stoic in difficult situations. Here are just a few examples of dicey situations we've experienced in the workplace:

- A candidate accepts a high-level position in the organization, only to change her mind the day before her start date.

- As an investigation is wrapping up, a witness comes forward with a completely contradictory statement about the alleged workplace harassment, pulling another team member into the situation.

- A high-potential employee placed in a new role quits on her third day.

- Sales numbers are unexpectedly low at the end of the quarter, and employees are running to HR, asking if the rumors are true—"Is our top competitor buying us out?"

Warriors have no way of scheduling these unexpected situations in their daily planners. You cannot simply set aside three to five o'clock every day as the "unpredictable" hours. You can have the best-laid plans, but it's guaranteed that something will interfere.

Accept that schedules will change. Some people can enter and leave Target in fifteen minutes, finding the five items on their shopping list with ease. But parents with children? You know how that can change plans. A quick pickup turns into a trip up and down every toy aisle, extra groceries, and a bathroom stop. Parents know what it means to be flexible and live in the "ish" time frame.

When the unpredictable occurs, take the time to do the job right. Re-adjust the priority list and move the new situation to the top. Bump everything else down one slot, and fully invest in this new scenario.

The Legal Battlefield

Now let's talk about something that has a polarizing effect on all employees: "the law."

Once HR has identified the root cause of a workplace conflict, it's not uncommon for "the law" to show up in the debrief and recommended solution. It's all too easy to fall back on the law for a quick and easy fix. And it's also a quick and easy way for HR to say no.

No, we cannot make changes to the prescreening process of candidates, because of the law. We cannot make changes to an employee's compensation program mid-year, because of wage and hour laws. We cannot fire an underperforming employee, because of discrimination laws.

Only HR Weenies shrug their shoulders, apologize, and point at the law. HR is an easy job when it's done by the law. HR Warriors, on the other hand, do not pass the buck. Warriors respect the law, and fully understand the ramifications if a company breaks it, but we work towards a solution while observing legalities.

Warriors have a great opportunity to demonstrate their mental agility and develop clever solutions to workplace problems, all while working within the boundaries of the law. A role in HR is difficult and time-consuming when done thoughtfully. Like surgeons, successful HR Warriors take on challenging cases. They do not shy away from complex scenarios, newly discovered diseases, or untested remedies.

The patient places trust in a surgeon's ability to remedy their pain, and employees place their trust in HR to resolve the workplace conflicts with hard work and cleverly devised solutions. Let's move beyond the days of using "the law" as the rationale for every decision we make.

WHEN KERI WORKED as a director in a large HR department that supported tens of thousands of employees across
the country, she and her team had to be keenly aware of
each state's employment laws. Not only that, but the mixed
employee base consisted of remote workers, temporary workers, and part-time and full-time workers, either salaried or
paid hourly. It was Keri's job to make sure her team gave the
legally correct advice to managers in the field.

There was no time for guessing, only getting work done.
This meant that providing accurate information was a must.
So, Keri managed a team (really, a team within a team) that
dealt only with employee relations issues. This was a small
team of in-house experts who could be reached any time,
whether during or after business hours, when the business
needed help.

This team doubled as a development opportunity for HR
generalists and performance consultants who wanted to
expand their knowledge base. The team went through intensive training to learn everything possible about employment
law, and went on to successfully support employees and
managers in all fifty states. And the business leaders were
positively gleeful, knowing they could simply send an email
or pick up the phone and talk to an expert. Tracking the ROI
of this team for the leadership became a key selling point
because Keri could prove that her team reduced legal risks
and saved managers time. A win-win!

AS AN HR WARRIOR, you will have a great opportunity to
demonstrate mental agility and create clever solutions to
workplace problems, while working within the boundaries of
the law. But let's be honest: most managers don't care about

the year the Lilly Ledbetter Fair Pay Act passed, the role of the Equal Employment Opportunity Commission, or the state differences in the Fair Labor Standards Act overtime requirements. What they do care about is whether they will lose their job for breaking a law. CEOs care if the company will have to litigate (and pay lots of money) for poor decisions. The PR Department cares if a news reporter shows up to question the company about claims of an unsafe work environment—and the potential public outcry.

This is not heartless, this is realistic. Because in any of these scenarios, a company that must financially remedy poor decisions may very well cost employees their jobs. Keeping this from happening is what you are paid to handle. You are not paid to make the CEO's decisions for them, but you *are* paid to predict potential roadblocks, illegal actions, and cultural clashes, and demonstrate with a keen ability how HR can head off the problem.

The executive team makes the executive decisions. HR identifies and removes the pain of detrimental decisions. The HR Warrior takes this responsibility seriously and has the heart to save the workplace.

Accuracy in the Workplace

As a practicing Warrior, you may hear from your clients (who could also be your business partners): "Thank you, you saved me!" or "What would we do without you?" or "I couldn't get through this without your coaching!" How great it feels to receive such praise—even though receiving compliments is not why Warriors fight. They are examples, however, of demonstrated Warrior status. Here's what to do to keep those compliments coming:

- Be accurate and identify the reason for an employee's pain. You are hired to find the root cause of the suffering and come up with a strategic way to make it all better. Get to the heart of the matter every day, in every situation.

- Do a root cause analysis rather than offering the magic pill of training to solve problems.

- Be curious. Ask questions and follow every lead to discover more information. The more information you can gather, the more intelligent recommendations you can make about any issue.

- Trust is essential. It takes time to build trust with business leaders and employees, especially when they have had bad experiences with HR in the past. Invest the time and effort to form a relationship, which is key to helping employees in any situation. Treat this bond with respect.

- Respect the law, but don't use it as an excuse to not act. The law is only a framework in which to operate, and Warriors find ways to solve problems with the help of the law, rather than relying on it.

- Get used to unpredictability. Remain steady and take the time required to find the right solution (not just the easy or the quick solution).

It's a good idea to keep tabs on how your business partners interact with you—it is a reflection of your level of accuracy. If you recognize any of the following signs, even in infancy, act quickly! (See "A Recap," below.) We've been scorched ourselves and want to help you never—ahem—feel the burn. So, what does it look like if someone in HR does not possess the quality of accuracy?

- You do not receive positive feedback or compliments from business partners. You receive only negative feedback about HR's role, or lack thereof.

- You are iced out. Your inbox is empty and your phone is not ringing. Your calendar is awfully light as well. When you take those two-hour lunches, no one misses you (or even notices you left). When you ask leaders if you can help them, they say, "No worries, I got it."

- Managers look for opportunities to set you up. Just like HR likes to pin the tail on the law, so our business partners want to pin the tail on HR. When something goes south, they have a way of maneuvering the situation to blame HR—"Sorry, they made me do it. Something about the law, they said." Uh-huh . . .

- Employees are never vulnerable around you. Instead, they want papers signed, policies updated, and a yes or no answer to their question. They don't seem to enjoy meeting with you or look forward to any check-ins. In fact, you never have any check-in meetings scheduled to talk with the employee base.

- You lack curiosity. You find out details of an HR situation after the fact: after an investigation, after someone is fired, after organizational changes.

- Managers lack trust in you. They are leery about being transparent in meetings when you are present.

- Every day looks the same. No crises, no challenges, no conundrums. You start work and leave work every day at the exact same time.

- Your career looks the same year after year after year. No new responsibilities, opportunities, or challenging work is presented to you.

A Recap

Warriors are ready to scrub in for surgery every day, because painful situations happen every day. Warriors are also adept at handling the emotional and psychological challenges of the workplace, with the most important factor in mind: people. We work in HR because we love and respect people. And this means we can have a significant impact on any organization. When you are working towards accuracy in your work, remember these points:

- Identify the pain points with a root cause analysis so they can be addressed.

- Be curious. The truth is often hidden.

- Build trust with employees.

- Prepare for unpredictable days while pursuing accuracy in your work.

- Take your time to find the solution.

- Avoid breaking the law, but be creative within its boundaries.

The trust you build with your clients as you help them win in the workplace is reward enough—when the business is successful, you are successful. And you fill your bank with a currency of goodwill, commitment, and reliability. Your bank account grows over time, and ultimately you will be able to purchase a much larger, strategic project—wait for the opportunity!

The Check-In

Now that you understand why being accurate is an essential quality of the HR Warrior, use these questions to reflect on your experience and help you grow your own accuracy:

- When is the last time you performed a root cause analysis?

- When did you propose a solution different from the one the client proposed?

- Think about your tendency to want to check the box or find a resolution. Do you want to do this quickly or slowly, and how does that impact your ability to be accurate?

- Do you like solving puzzles and figuring out the why? If yes, keep doing it at work; if no, talk or partner with people who love puzzles. Get into their head, so to speak, and learn.

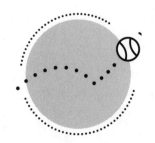

CHARGE

CHAPTER 6
R Is for Resiliency

"YOU DIDN'T GET THE JOB." That is what Keri heard after pursuing a promotion for months. She had worked as an HR director and was looking at the title of vice-president for her next role. It was the next step in her career, and one for which she had spent the last several years preparing. She earned her PhD, achieved industry certifications, built and led a highly successful HR team, established strong relationships with key members of the leadership team, and was now ready for more. But the job was given to a candidate from outside the organization.

Keri felt frustrated, to say the least. But she did have another project to add to her plate: building an HR team that could flawlessly execute enterprise-wide change management initiatives. Instead of turning down this opportunity—it was extra work for her and her team—she knew it would make her grow both personally and professionally. The work meant additional exposure for her team, and more opportunities for her to partner with senior leadership on high-priority needs. What else could she learn? What else could she add to her résumé?

Although Keri did not acquire the title of VP initially, another title was added to her current role: Director of Change Management. This role gave her an opportunity to acquire even more new knowledge than the VP role would have offered. Sometimes there is a good reason you don't get what you wanted; you just can't see it at the time. This experience helped Keri move into bigger and better jobs.

SOMETIMES IN LIFE we get knocked down. This never feels good. But it can feel especially painful in your career, because most people have a natural tendency to want to achieve more (that's why you are reading this book). In this chapter, we discuss why resilience is such an important quality for an HR Warrior. Put on those boxing gloves!

For an HR Warrior, here's what to keep in mind when it comes to resiliency:

- You will get knocked down as you develop your Warrior skills. That's okay—always get back up.

- Having a thick skin is a requirement. Without it, the level of influence you will have on your clients and the company will be minimal.

- Achieving resilience takes time—be in it for the long haul.

- You are not alone. Rely on teammates, mentors, and partners for the encouragement you need to build the resiliency muscle.

Get Back Up!

Remember when children's playgrounds were filled with monkey bars, sandboxes, jungle gyms, and those metal spinners that made you feel slightly nauseated? Recess usually left children with muddy jeans and possibly a few scrapes. The one key to any successful recess was this: Keep playing! Don't quit until the school bell called you to class. If you fall, get back up! It was great preparation for adulthood.

Maybe you are better at the monkey bars now that you are an adult, but there are still lots of ways we get knocked down. You go through a painful breakup because the person you thought was forever turns out to be a temporary high. Get back up! You diet and lose five pounds, then when the holidays come around, you put on six. Get back up! You experience an unexpected layoff at a company that you have remained loyal to for ten years. Get back up! Recognize the theme?

Learning how to persevere is a prerequisite for adulthood, like learning how to separate clothes in the laundry pile, and how to load a dishwasher. Perseverance is a quality that should be woven into your career in both subtle and obvious ways. Practicing perseverance in an HR career is no exception. Indeed, it is a requirement.

We've mentioned how deeply emotions are embedded in the work of Human Resources, and that means your own emotions as well as those of your clients and their employees. As representatives of HR, you have a more intimate interaction than most with people in the workplace, and that can prove challenging at times. Orchestrating a mass layoff, downgrading employees' benefits plans, or delivering a performance warning tests even the most experienced professional. But perseverance functions like the eye of the storm—it is the calm when everything around you is spinning out of control.

HR experiences good and bad days. The good days are amazingly rewarding—interviewing the perfect candidate for the high-profile job opening, extending a lavish compensation package, and hearing a resounding "I accept" in response makes for a great day! Unfortunately, good days are always counterbalanced by bad ones. Such as the day you are in a room with a thirty-year employee, a severance package on the table in front of him. Or the day you hear that the company isn't doing well and there will be no merit pay or bonuses. Those make for heart-wrenching moments.

Monica remembers one bad day in particular. She was working with a small team of HR professionals who were on a tight schedule to carry out one-on-one layoff conversations with a group of employees. These layoffs had been diligently planned, and the selection process had been scrutinized. Although the process would be handled with the utmost care and respect for the employees, it was still an awful experience. Monica remembers walking towards the conference room for her first conversation, the employee, a man who looked to be within a few years of retirement, standing nervously by the door with pen and small notebook in hand. He tucked his shirt into his pants as if to tidy himself up, brushed his short hair towards his ears, and stood up straight. He had no idea what was about to happen. Monica wanted to turn around and run in the other direction.

The emotional highs and lows of an HR career can be challenging, but you should persevere to strike a balance between good and bad days. The day after a challenging layoff conversation, you might have an opportunity to discuss the immense progress of a manager who is fighting for her next promotion. Focusing on the positive days can help counterbalance the negative ones.

Unfortunately, bad days arrive unexpectedly. No surprise, but not everyone likes HR. And sometimes those who do not like HR set the cultural tone for the entire company. Occasionally, business leaders will show disdain for HR, to the point that the HR budget gets slashed. Some leaders feel that HR departments like Organization Development or Talent Development are expendable when the bottom line is not as healthy as anticipated. This can come as a big blow to the strategies of any HR team. How do you drive home the importance of development plans for employees if you don't have in-house experts? As difficult as the situation is, you make it work.

For example, when the company doesn't have talent development experts on board, HR generalists can learn new skills. The Benefits, Compensation, and Employee Relations employees can get in on the fun too, turning lemons into lemonade.

Let's look at an example. After spending six weeks developing a sales-specific training course within your HR team, the leader of the five-day class—and the most recognizable face of the sales leadership team—quits. He took another job, at your competitor, and you've got no one to lead the class. Thirty sales executives from across the country are waiting for the hotel shuttle to pick them up and bring them to headquarters. What do you do?

You might want to call the CEO and express your frustration. If you do, be professional about it. Situations like this come up frequently in HR, because you see a side of employees no one else does. It can be difficult to walk down the hallways and cross paths with an employee who is currently under investigation for lewd behavior towards a coworker. But when you do, you keep calm, look down at your cell phone as if you just received an important text, and don't flinch as you pass by.

Develop the resiliency to not react emotionally. Instead, ask yourself if there is another solution. Perhaps there is another sales leader who would love the development opportunity to lead this training class. Lemonade.

What if the company leadership just doesn't like HR? They view the department as old-fashioned, traditional, out-of-touch, or like the annoying parents in the room who don't let the kids have any fun. Rules, rules, rules! You get shuffled to the sidelines and don't get a chance to play very often. You are copied on emails passively, included only as "optional" participants in department meetings, or simply get a heads-up summary after important business decisions are made. They might be thinking, "Why include HR in the planning process? They don't provide any insight or creative solutions!" But HR Warriors can offer these things. And more importantly, they want to participate.

One struggle many HR departments face is the perception gap. The perception gap can create many bad days in the office. You can still have good days working within an organization that doesn't see the potential of HR, or doesn't want to use your skill set. And slowly and surely, you will find ways to benefit others.

Attend that meeting for which you are listed as an optional participant. Take thorough notes. And before the meeting is over, provide one helpful suggestion. Question one idea. Take a chance. Be bold. Showcase in a ten-second way what you bring to the table. And tomorrow, build on that. Find a new

Resiliency is shown through **perseverance.** And perseverance is shown through **consistency.**

way to influence the workplace. Send an encouraging email to a manager who made a tough decision. Acknowledge the success of a fellow professional's recent training class.

No matter what obstacle is thrown your way in the workplace, find a way to fight through it. Day by day, we show up. Resiliency is shown through perseverance. And perseverance is shown through consistency. Brush off the dirt from your knees and keep at it!

Develop a Thick Skin

During the time that Keri held the job titles of HR Director and Director of Change Management, she had to work with numerous outside consultants to execute the company's plans. One organization did not mesh well with Keri.

Conflict is inevitable in this kind of situation. An outside firm will often clash with those who work in the company, especially when it comes to the roles and responsibilities of the employees. Keri and a member of her team created strategies on how to carry out an enterprise-wide organizational change, but the consultancy group had very specific ideas on how to manage this creation process. And process was key—these people loved process! They loved assembling spreadsheets, reports, numbers, data, and documentation that took a significant amount of time to complete. Keri and her team wanted to get to work.

Ah, the balance between documenting the process and taking action.

The consultants wanted full control and were not interested in partnering with HR (sound familiar?). They were the "experts" and needed little input from an HR team, which they believed didn't know much about change management. Keri interpreted their actions like this: challenge accepted. She met their deadlines week after week. When they asked for documentation, she worked over the weekend to deliver what they wanted by Monday morning. She created processes, she accurately recorded the workload and tasks, just as they asked. She was a true partner, but she would still get the work done.

By the end of this project, the business was happy. Keri's colleague remarked, "This is the best change management I have ever seen." Outcome achieved. Keri didn't let the process bring her down; she rose to the challenge. And the greatest of all the challenges was to get the desired result for the business. On the plus side, the outside consultants did not remain working for the company much longer. Keri was happy with that outcome! (We're still human, after all.)

HOW DO YOU BUILD resilience every day? With small wins and by having a thick skin. This doesn't just mean that you keep a positive attitude. It also means having a deep, strong, gut-check response to bad days in the workplace. When the company leadership does not value HR, this is a challenge. But remember that the leadership is not your enemy. You are on the same team, and you can find creative ways to showcase your abilities.

Deliver feedback on a PowerPoint presentation. Respond to a mass email with a positive idea for the workplace culture (even when no one else hits the Reply All button with worthy commentary). Attend the next town hall meeting and be brave enough to ask a question. A question that will benefit someone, challenge the status quo, encourage a team. Show those leaders what you can do!

And on those challenging days, if you need to step away from your desk and head outside for ten minutes, do it. If you need to phone a friend or family member to vent, do it—just remember to do it somewhere private. Warriors are not without emotions, but Warriors do not let emotions stop them from accomplishing goals. Develop a thick skin through simple, daily steps, and you're making progress.

MONICA DID NOT HAVE a thick skin when she started in HR. She would consider herself a conflict-avoider: Can't we all just get along? Besides, it sucks telling people what they don't want to hear.

But in HR, she quickly learned that she had to deliver bad news, sometimes far too frequently. On one occasion, she had to share negative feedback with a director on her interviewing skills. Enough candidates and enough Talent Acquisition

Warriors are not without emotions, but Warriors **do not let emotions stop them from accomplishing goals.**

employees had shared their concerns with Monica that she had to take the next step of providing constructive feedback to the director.

Monica wrestled with this for several days. What would the director's reaction be? How could Monica couch the feedback in a way that would not upset the director? Would the feedback come as a total surprise? Monica practiced what she would say, how she would say it, what her tone would be. And eventually, the time to make the phone call arrived. She spent roughly seven minutes of the call inching towards and around the feedback she needed to deliver. And then, suddenly, the conversation turned.

"Monica, if you have something to say, just say it. You're beating around the bush."

The director called her out, and rightfully so.

"Fair enough," said Monica. "I've received feedback that those who partner with you are struggling to move candidates through the hiring process when you are involved." There it was. Feedback delivered. The director appreciated Monica's candor, and Monica appreciated hers. Moving forward, the two had a well-balanced working relationship because they trusted that each would speak truthfully and be receptive to feedback, whether good or bad.

Monica's skin grew a little thicker that day. She needed to hear the truth about her hesitancy from the director, and it helped her improve as an HR professional. Sharing that feedback with the director also helped her improve her hiring skills.

AS WE MENTIONED, resilience is displayed through perseverance. Developing a thick skin also involves perseverance. Even if you have the full backing of the entire organization, there are circumstances that still have an impact on what we do every day. When the economy takes a dive, businesses must scale back. Programs, training, and extra benefits can be erased quicker than the wrong answers on a chalkboard. Suddenly the workplace feels more like boarding school—minimalist, strict, and uniform. That's not fun. If there's anything we know, working in HR, it's that we play in the culture sandbox daily. We can help strategize, shape, shift, and share the culture of the organization. When the employees are down, make sure you have a thick enough skin to pick them back up!

Which brings to mind an old saying having to do with silver linings...

Although HR is not the cheerleader of the company, you can be cheerful. Despite the frustrations, fear, and phobias circling around the watercooler, you can advance an agenda that employees can be excited about. What about creating a webinar course on leadership principles that doesn't cost the company any money but which can be shared with a group of employees aspiring towards a promotion? Even if external pressures are making it hard for the workplace, and its employees, to be successful, you can display motivation, drive, and determination to improve the environment. And you need to have a thick skin to do just that.

Building Resiliency Is a Process

Occasionally, having a thick skin looks like nothing at all: no reaction, no response, no gut response to an awful decision. The decisions our leaders and clients make are not always welcome, because HR can foresee the results—the ugly, ill-timed, detrimental results. You try to sway leadership towards making a good choice, at least from HR's vantage point, but this doesn't always happen.

You must still drive the business agenda forward, and this requires resilience. You can't protest or chain yourself to the cafeteria table. You can't storm the podium at the quarterly investors meeting, or wear black T-shirts to work every single day in protest. At times, HR Warriors must do absolutely nothing and let the chips fall where they may.

Often the best changes in any organization move slightly faster than a sloth climbing a tree and coincidentally (or maybe not) the slowness often coincides with the size of the organization. Achievement takes time. Runners can't train for a marathon by running a five-mile route once. Chefs don't open a restaurant after they learn to boil water. Surgeons don't open their own practice after they earn an A in anatomy. Becoming an expert takes practice.

Remember our story of Monica's reluctance to share feedback? The first time she did share it, it was hard. But through consistent practice, you can become an expert at giving feedback. Okay, maybe that's not a top entry on your goals list. Who wants to tout that they are an expert at giving feedback? But these small behaviors, practiced consistently over time, are what turn a Weenie into a Warrior.

Early in any career, it can be difficult to make the right decision in a new situation. First-time managers experience this often. The first one-on-one meeting with an employee who is struggling with their workload is never easy. But managers do learn how to effectively communicate and are better for it when the next challenging conversation comes around.

Developing resilience is not simply responding calmly, or not responding, to a particular string of events. You'll encounter a lot of emotions in this line of work—coming at you from all angles—which is why emotional resiliency is important. And since much of your work is confidential and therefore cannot be discussed openly, you'll need to rely on your fellow HR partners, those other will-be Warriors, for help in difficult times. Building camaraderie with teammates is helpful when it comes to managing our emotions. So go ahead, offer advice, or words of encouragement, and remain open to the support offered to you.

When it's eight o'clock at night and you're still at the office, updating the retention rates one more time, remember: You're not alone. You may feel that you're alone. You might crank the *Rocky* theme music through your computer speakers and imagine yourself in the gray jumpsuit running up a set of stairs, dripping with sweat. And that kind of "getting psyched" activity can draw a certain emotion out of a person when they need it. When you may be on the verge of quitting, when you may be frustrated beyond belief, finding ways to motivate yourself does help. But the moment fades, and the problem, the frustrations, the anxiety, remain. More than a catchy soundtrack, what you need is emotional resilience.

Consider these situations (all of which have happened to us):

- An investigation drags on for six weeks because more and more anonymous complaints come forth about a call center manager with a fifty-employee team.

- A surprise Equal Employment Opportunity Commission audit is ordered, right in the middle of transitioning to a new ATS that will now, for the first time, track diverse applicants.

- A thirty-person department is laid off within a six-hour time frame.

Those are difficult workplace scenarios, and HR must not only manage the process but also manage emotions throughout the process. HR is privy to information that the employee base is not and, as such, our work is highly confidential. But this confidentiality can create challenges. We find out information before other employees do. A reduction of the workforce must be planned weeks, sometimes months, in advance, and during that time we carry around a list of who is on the list. That is tough.

When an employee is placed on a performance improvement plan, HR knows because they have been speaking with the manager about the employee's low performance. When this occurs concurrently with that employee asking HR for career guidance about another position in the organization they want to apply for—well, that is awkward.

When benefit changes are scheduled for the next calendar year that will affect families with a health savings account, and an employee comes into the office asking for paperwork to fill out for a surgery planned for January, that is painful.

Sometimes a difficult moment turns into a difficult year. Keri has worked with leaders who needed a lot of coaching to realize the impact of a poor performer on their team. Oftentimes in HR, we recognize the impact of a poor performer before the manager does. Team morale starts to drop (and concerned conversations with HR increase). Team performance decreases, gossiping and watercooler talk increase, and a lack of team cohesiveness becomes visible to those on the outside.

Keri shared her feedback about the poor performer with the manager. She had the difficult conversation but, for various reasons, the manager didn't want to take action. Maybe the employee *seemed* to perform well. Maybe the employee said all the right things. Maybe the employee had critical and "irreplaceable" skills that the manager was concerned about losing from his team.

Ultimately, it is the manager's decision to address performance issues. HR can only do so much. Sometimes Keri felt she was not making any progress. One, two, three conversations with the manager later and the employee was still having a negative impact on the manager's team. And, at a certain point, the manager didn't want to hear about these concerns from Keri anymore.

Keri realized that the key to addressing the manager's reluctance was rather simple yet powerful: remain optimistic. Continue to work with the manager. Continue to problem-solve, provide support on various initiatives, discuss team performance. Keep the conversation going. This is how Keri learned to bounce back—and you can too, whatever your situation. Be resilient, and trust that the honest conversations will eventually make progress. And whatever you do, do not give up.

When you are developing resiliency, you may be tempted to make changes that will not be in your best interests later. We may be tempted to take drastic steps to make our voices heard, or to take drastic actions to change the environment. Work on shrugging off the following temptations:

- To change jobs. When a role isn't working out, you may have a flight rather than fight mentality. Fight! (Unless the company's values do not align with your own, which is a different situation.)

- To change managers. If you disagree with your higher-up, the temptation is to look for a leader who will agree with you. Stay the course. (Unless the manager demonstrates behaviors or asks you to do things that conflict with your values.)

- To change your mindset. You may feel that an improvement in your career or in the environment is taking too long. Don't throw in the towel; wait a little longer.

- To change behaviors. Although some people may not deserve your respect, and you might feel the need to make that known, remain professional—always.

Resilience weaves through everything HR Warriors do. And resilience is demonstrated through consistent effort and a consistently positive attitude, brought to work every day like a lunch pail. High and low days, big or skeletal budgets, leadership support or disapproval: all the peaks and valleys offer us a chance to develop resilience.

Resiliency in the Workplace

Chin up. Becoming an HR Warrior is not for the faint of heart! But you need to build resiliency into your plan of attack, and especially when facing complicated HR situations. Unfortunately, some responses to complicated HR situations hamper the growth of resiliency. Here are key ways to ensure your resiliency grows:

Resilience weaves through everything HR Warriors do.

- Resist the temptation to be discouraged. There are plenty of reasons to feel frustrated, that you are stalled or even hindered in your efforts. Find the good in any situation and build on it.

- Find your own equilibrium. Emotions run high in the workplace. Walk through the halls of any company and you will hear little except the clicking of a computer mouse and the taps of typing on a keyboard. But beneath the quiet surface, loud and rowdy emotions are lurking. Stay centered.

- Accept that emotions are a part of the human experience. Employees don't expect HR Warriors to be emotionless. Build trust with employees, and be willing to be vulnerable and transparent.

- Take the work one day at a time. Small daily habits can lead to big results!

Sometimes runners don't cross the finish line, chefs are criticized for less than perfect plates, and archers have the audience ducking behind bushes for protection. It's clear when individuals are not successful in their craft, and this goes for those in HR too. So, what does it look like when a would-be Warrior has not developed the needed level of resilience?

- Emotions are in full force at work. Crying, yelling, and knee-jerk sarcasm with employees and clients are visible and unrestrained.

- You feel like you're riding a roller coaster. Inconsistency in performance is a daily reality. One day they are excited to be planning next year's training budget, the next day they look as if they should call in sick with a stress-related illness.

- Delivering a highly successful and impactful training class is followed up by a lack of diligence to track the training budget. A passion to help employees create career goals is exchanged for a lack of interest to provide documentation to HR leaders about the employee's progress.

- Quitting. Quitting the project team, quitting the role, quitting the company. People searching for greener pastures may believe that another company or another manager or another, fully funded HR Department will solve all their problems. They abandon ship with the first sign of a cloud in the sky.

A Recap

We all need to develop a level of resiliency for facing life's challenges, and that includes the challenges in our careers. The wonderful thing about working in HR is that there is ample opportunity to demonstrate resiliency.

The key takeaways from this chapter are:

- You will get knocked down as you develop your Warrior skills. That's okay—get back up!

- Having a thick skin is a requirement. Without it, the level of influence you will have on your clients and the company will be minimal.

- Find balance between your own emotions and working towards a solution. Embrace how you feel and determine how it can be turned into an actionable plan.

- Achieving resilience takes time—be in it for the long haul.

- You are not alone. Rely on teammates, mentors, and partners to find the encouragement you need to build the resiliency muscle.

The Check-In

There is a saying: "Do not compare your beginning to someone else's middle." In other words, be okay with being a novice, and be okay with knowing you need to improve certain skills. No one shows up to a job on the first day knowing everything and with 100 percent resiliency. No one can predict the fallout of every situation. Not even CEOs have that luxury. You can always find others who are smarter, more talented, and more accomplished than you. The key is to enjoy being surrounded by such people—and together foster your growth.

Consider these questions in thinking about your current level of resiliency:

1. What is one of the most difficult challenges you have faced in your career?

2. In what ways did you demonstrate resilience during those challenges?

3. Looking back now, could you have improved your responses?

4. What can you do in your current job to develop additional resiliency?

Achieving resilience takes time—be in it for the long haul.

CHAR**G**E

CHAPTER 7
G Is for
Goal-Oriented

WHEN MONICA STARTED working in HR, the first manager she ever had taught her a huge lesson about understanding the company's business goals. Only a few weeks into her new HR role, Monica was partnering with a hiring manager about a problem she was having with a recruiter. "She's not presenting good candidates to me, and it's been dragging on far too long," complained the hiring manager. Monica took notes, asked the manager detailed questions, and made sure she understood the manager's frustrations. Simple enough.

Monica talked to her manager about the exchange, and explained to him her plan of attack. (Monica had learned early on that with her manager, you do not reverberate a problem, you state your problem and propose solutions.) She planned to have a conversation with the recruiter to stress the importance of open communication and regular feedback to the hiring manager about the recruiting progress on a weekly basis.

Monica felt pretty good about things. One of her first HR problems solved! The hiring manager also felt good about Monica's plan, and so she patted herself on the back. But then Monica's manager asked an important but previously overlooked question: "Does she need to hire a branch manager?"

It was a good question. Monica had never thought to ask the hiring manager why she felt the need to hire for this position. She assumed that the manager needed the role, so it was her job to help get it filled. But therein lay Monica's lack of understanding about the financial and organizational implications of hiring a manager-level employee.

"Well, I assume so—" Monica answered.

"Never assume" was her manager's answer. "The regional team recently shared with all the offices that because of last quarter's performance, any additional spend would be difficult to gain approval for. Did you get approval for this role?"

Monica had not considered the bigger picture: the consequences of hiring a manager-level position when the region was struggling financially. After further due diligence, and an uncomfortable conversation with the hiring manager, Monica discovered that a branch manager located forty-five miles away would be able to cover both branches with minimal additional work. And it would provide a terrific development opportunity for that branch manager.

Monica learned later that the top goal of the regional team was to save money over the coming quarter. Partnering with the hiring manager to keep her aligned with the region's goals was a better solution than trying to close the gap on the time to fill metric. For Monica, this situation was an excellent lesson in understanding the business's goals and how she could help her business partners achieve them.

ALTHOUGH RESILIENCY IS VITAL to the success of an HR Warrior, in many ways it fosters and enhances the HR Warrior quality of being goal-oriented, both personally and professionally. In this chapter, we explore how staying focused on business goals is essential for the HR Warrior. Here's what you need to know:

- Understand that the company's goals are the Warriors' goals. When you become deeply knowledgeable about what your company is trying to accomplish, you are the most effective in your own role.

- Be a constant learner. This is how you can remain accurate and make an impact as you grow in your career.

- Strategy counts in an emotion-filled workplace. Warriors acknowledge and accept tumultuous environments, but they focus on the goals despite them.

The Business Goals Are HR's Goals

Understand the company's goals, even if employees don't. And even if the business leaders don't think HR needs to understand the business goals.

HR is commonly referred to as a support or admin function (i.e., we are not a revenue-generating function like sales). This means that some business leaders view HR as a drain on the company's bank account. The perception is that although HR does not contribute their fair share to the business, we still like to tell employees what they can and cannot do.

In the 2005 *Fast Company* article "Why We Hate HR," author Keith H. Hammonds, quoting Anthony J. Rucci, executive vice-president of health-care supply distributor Cardinal Health, writes:

> Most human-resources managers aren't particularly interested in, or equipped for, doing business. And in a business, that's sort of a problem. As guardians of a company's talent, HR has to understand how people serve corporate objectives. Instead, "business acumen is the single biggest factor that HR professionals in the U.S. lack today."[1]

Rucci refers to "business acumen," but we argue that what he is talking about is not general business acumen. It is great that you can read a P&L statement, but if you cannot understand what that P&L says about the current state of your company, it's worthless.

If you work for a public company, you can read press releases and investor relations information on your company website. What is the stock price? How is the price today compared with that in the past? What are competitor companies' stock prices? You can look at what the earnings have been, quarter over quarter, for the last year. You can review the revenue generated, as compared with that of competitors. You don't need to have a finance degree to understand how your company is performing financially.

But what does knowing the stock price of your company have to do with your HR job, you might ask. A lot!

Understanding the environment your business is operating within will help you perform stronger. No one works for free. Every employee, from the CEO to the accountant, wants

---

1 Keith H. Hammonds, "Why We Hate HR," *Fast Company,* August 1, 2005, https://www.fastcompany.com/53319/why-we-hate-hr.

a paycheck. And employees might not get merit pay, bonuses, or a 401k match, and they may even lose their jobs, if the company is not profitable. By understanding the financial status, you can understand what frustrations or challenges the leadership team face. You can understand why a round of layoffs may occur, and why hiring is put on ice, and when managers must stay within a certain budget when responding to unexpected attrition.

Empathy—the ability to identify with the feelings, thoughts, and attitudes of others—will help you effectively respond to employees' emotional reactions to the organization's decisions. And a sound knowledge of the company's fiscal challenges can help you do that.

IN ONE OF HER ROLES, Keri worked closely with the leader of a North American division that supported thousands of employees in every US state. A significant pain point for this leader was his need to get more out of his sales organization. He wanted stronger sales results in an increasingly competitive industry, and he expressed his angst about this to Keri on a few (which is to say, a lot of) occasions: What needs to happen for our sales professionals to get better results? How do we hold them accountable for poor results? How do I know whether we are hiring the right level of talent to help us achieve our goals? All great questions.

To find the answers, Keri and her team partnered with the sales leaders on a plan to:

1. Understand the sales goals. What are the expectations of the sales leaders? What are acceptable results and nonacceptable results? How do you hold employees accountable?

2. Document the standards. Keri's team spent time documenting the answers to these questions, to ensure that every employee was held to the same standard, and that employees understood the expectations.

3. Create a solution-selling program for the entire sales staff. Interviews indicated that the sales executives had not received any formal training on how to solution-sell; thus, this training was critical to the new standards set by the leadership team and not just a magic pill (see page 94 for a discussion of training as a "magic pill").

4. Track the ROI. It would be impossible to know if training was effective if Keri did not define what the ROI should look like, and measure those results for months after the training was complete.

Here's the twist: there was no ROI in the solution-selling program. The training didn't seem to be effective. Keri worked with the VP of Sales to conduct another root cause analysis and find an outside expert consultant who could identify the areas needing improvement. This consultant partnered with Keri and her team to identify the root cause of the lacking sales results: the sales team had learned a graduate-level course of solution selling, when first they needed the elementary education.

Keri knew the sales organization had to build a strong foundation before it could excel. The improved selling program was revamped to teach the basics, and when Keri's team tracked the new ROI, they found that this time the results were stronger. The company leadership embraced the training program and the HR professionals who had helped them reach their business goals.

Unfortunately, there are some HR professionals who simply memorize the business language. They know the buzzwords ("Our burning platform is . . ."); they know the financials ("Our shareholder value dramatically increased!"); they know the operations ("Let's put a project plan together . . ."); but that doesn't mean they understand the business in any meaningful way.

These are the coworkers who enter a team meeting and begin whiteboarding schematic plans to reinvent the talent strategy. Tossing around business lingo they read in *Forbes*, they say things like "Let's *capitalize on opportunities* to *identify talent gaps* and create *a workforce strategy* that will turn this company around!" But they don't truly understand the environment.

You've probably seen this kind of coworker in action. You know, that same HR director who has yet to address their own budget—one that is in the red.

No one likes a fake. Especially when jobs, careers, and opportunities are on the line. Where business goals are concerned, don't fake it until you make it. HR business partners like to talk business talk. You feel like you are at the cool kids' table, and on point with the trends. But there is a difference between speaking the strategy and understanding the strategy. Figure out the difference early on, and you will benefit for years to come.

Understanding the business goals is not about adding to your professional knowledge bank but about the role you play in the greater success of the company. Rather than focusing on sounding smart by saying the right phrases at the right moments (and in front of the right people), slow down. Learn about the business so that when you can contribute, you do so in a truly beneficial way.

Understanding the business goals is not about adding to your professional knowledge bank but **about the role you play in the greater success of the company.**

Here is a list of pertinent questions that every HR business partner should be able to answer about the company:

- What is the leadership team trying to achieve in the next three, six, nine months?

- What are the business segments that the company is measured on (financials, operations, sales, marketing, talent)?

- What are the metrics that are measuring the success or failure of each major segment of the strategic plan?

- What is the long-term plan for the company? Does the company want to make an IPO, to be acquired, or reach a certain revenue level?

- How does the company plan to reach its goals (new product offerings, organic growth, acquisition, etc.)?

- What are the internal and external challenges that could inhibit the company from reaching its goals?

You should be able to answer these questions without looking up information or turning to resources. (Okay, maybe that's a stretch, especially with the financial and operational metrics-driven questions.) But at least have an idea about what your leaders are thinking, and worrying, about every day. The HR Warrior knows the answer to these questions, and that is how they can influence and impact the results of the company goals.

The Constant Learner

To be goal-oriented in a way that benefits your organization, and your career, you must always be open to learning. Even though we (well, most of us) are not in school anymore, that doesn't give you an excuse not to learn. Granted, we don't arrive at work like we did school (no assigned classroom desks, and no eighty-pound backpacks), but we should arrive at work ready to learn just the same.

Learning is growth. And if our companies want to grow, its employees must continue learning. Like muscles when you don't use them, opportunities will shrink and eventually disappear if you aren't upgrading and renewing your skill set. And HR Warriors want to be the ripped people of HR!

What are we supposed to learn, you ask? As an HR professional, you must first and foremost learn about the business, both internally and externally, you work for.

Internally, you need to understand the business model of your company:

- How is it organizationally structured?

- What is the company's mission and values (why do we do what we do)?

- How does it make money? (Understanding its profitability.)

- What do we offer? What are the company's products and services?

Externally, you need to understand the company's competition:

- Who are the direct and indirect competitors in the marketplace, and why?

- How is the business doing against its competitors? What is its position?

- What is happening economically, socially, and in the field of technology that will have an impact on the business?

- What are the differentiators? What does the business have that others do not that makes it successful?

That's a lot to learn. Don't drink from the firehose—you don't need to understand all of this by eight o'clock Monday morning! Some of this information will come to you if you simply pay attention in meetings and read all the company-wide emails that are distributed. Executives want buy-in from employees, and they will be especially pleased when HR takes a vested interest in what is happening in all segments of the business.

You don't need to create flash cards and obsessively test yourself each night. Just be curious. Be present during the workday. Review company-wide information. Read online sources about the industry and your company's competitors, and economic news. Read magazines, newspapers, and industry journals. Check out the websites and press releases of other companies in the industry. Sign up for emails with industry updates.

Spend thirty minutes each week studying. (And do not ask if this can be paid time—focus, future Warrior, this is about your career!) The more your knowledge about your business increases, the more opportunities will come your way.

Emotions Run High

Keri, as HR director, and her team were once partnered with the new VP of the company's West Coast division to address the talent of the VP's team. In the first of multiple twelve-hour-day planning meetings, the goal was to come up with a talent strategy that would elevate the business results. This was a "roll up your sleeves and brainstorm on a blank sheet of paper"-type meeting.

As the meeting progressed, the team realized that a high-profile client of the VP's division, a California-based client, was on the brink of being lost. The client wanted a strong leader who could be on-site daily to oversee and rebuild the operation, but the VP's current team was not operating up to this client's standards.

The VP wanted HR on the front lines. She needed Keri and her team to identify the right talent that could crush it in this temporary leadership role—and as soon as possible, to prevent losing the client. An additional pressure was that, although the senior vice-president placed significant trust in Keri's team, thanks to their consistently strong results, he was still anxious that the crucial needs of the company's high-profile client be addressed. Keri and her team spent several days dissecting the leadership role in question to determine its priorities, the changes that needed to be made, and what actions would increase the operational efficiency on-site.

In an unexpected twist, the HR manager, who was also in attendance at the meetings, was eventually identified as the right person for the role. The unconventional answer had been right in front of everyone! Thankfully, the VP was willing to think outside the box and trust such a recommendation. The HR manager was well experienced with the goals of the business and those of the client, and could articulate them in order to help the company succeed.

Risk-taking has its place, and in this situation, the ability of the VP and Keri to think outside the HR box led to a creative solution that exceeded expectations. But what did other

leaders in the company say about the selection of this particular candidate for the leadership role? "Is HR now running
client programs?" "Why is HR involved in operations?" "Are
they really paid to do that?"

This situation was an opportunity for Keri to show her
company that HR had skin in the game. Keri's team was truly
invested in helping the company succeed, and could do so by
demonstrating awareness of the client's pain points, solving
performance concerns by identifying talent, and measuring
the ROI. And there was a bonus: not only was the new leadership role an outstanding development opportunity for the HR
manager, but his stepping into this temporary new role meant
greater responsibilities for others. HR proved to the company
that they help the division achieve its business goals directly,
rather than indirectly.

EMOTIONS ARE A HOT-BUTTON issue for the HR Warrior. It's
immensely important to acknowledge that the actions HR
must take will often be sensitive, confidential, or uncomfortable in nature, or a combination of the three. Time to pull up
the big kid pants and resolve the issues so that business goals
can be met. That's what the company pays you to do.

In the example above of Keri's experience with the California client, the business goals were at stake and emotions
were running at a high. The VP felt pressure from the client
and from the Sales VP. The HR manager felt nervous about
taking on such a huge responsibility. The client was put off by
the initial suggestion that an HR professional be the one stepping in to solve the operational problems.

Emotions lead us in a specific direction, and not always in
the right one. Companies don't base their business goals on
feelings. As HR Warriors, once we understand our companies'

goals, we need to present solutions to problems while working through the emotional aspects. In Keri's case, despite all the emotions involved, she and her team took the time necessary to understand the VP's goals, in the end delivering an unconventional but effective solution. That doesn't mean people's emotions went away but, in this instance, they did not prevent the company from achieving its business goals.

As we've said, HR deals in part with the unpredictable side of the business: people and their emotions. You are not approached by management when the EBITDA is not included in the monthly financials, or when the company's brand typeface has not been incorporated into the newest online banner ad. Those instances, as those in HR jokingly say, are the unemotional part of the business. But if someone is going to be hired, fired, promoted, retired, or placed on a performance plan, guess who must answer that call? HR. We are in the people business.

Do not let an uncomfortable or emotional situation keep you from acting. Employees may hesitate to speak with HR because it's a personal situation and you are a stranger to them. Clients may be facing a tricky employee relations issue and feel nervous about talking with you because you are a stranger to them too. But what will bridge the gap from stranger to problem solver is your ability to deliver a clearly defined action plan.

Strategy Counts

Keri had the opportunity to lead her team, including Monica, to develop a new business strategy that would have an impact on an entire US-based organization, consisting of 1,800 employees. No small task! The task required an incredible amount of change management in order to design a new organizational structure, and the business leader felt confident Keri, Monica, and the rest of her team could lead this change initiative. They had a lot of work ahead of them, not only in the change management process but in all HR processes, such as interview processes, hiring criteria, compensation plans, updating job descriptions, new leadership transitions, and so on.

The organizational change required all existing employees to change jobs—and that is no joke. The company needed to create an entirely new business model, which meant that the roles and responsibilities of all employees needed to change. For every US-based market, the HR team needed to create a strategy that would encompass all employees understanding the new roles and applying for those roles that interested them, interviewing for those positions, and then possibly being rehired under a new compensation plan, which could include relocation packages and different benefits. The HR team was interviewing late into the night in each of these markets.

Together, Keri, Monica, and the rest of the team worked constantly for several weeks to design HR processes and strategize about how best to deliver them with the least disruption to the business and still with respect for every employee. Maximum brainpower (fueled by late-night snacks and energy drinks) went into the planning sessions. And although there were a few hiccups in each market, they kept their eyes on the goal: to implement the new organizational structure and ensure every single employee had the chance to start fresh in the job of their choice.

You can only imagine the level of emotion all employees, in each market, might have felt knowing they now had to interview for jobs when they had securely held one just the day before. Keri's team kept at it day after day, following the designed processes and managing the emotions of all employees. The HR team understood what the business goals were, and that their strategy was to act on it.

Throughout this massive change management project, the team tracked the progress of clearly defined action steps:

1. They created an HR scorecard to define actions and track results; this scorecard was updated monthly and reviewed with the leaders each quarter.

2. They did not hide the results of the scorecard. If items were in red because tasks were not completed on time, Keri marked her team red, as in: incomplete and behind schedule. They remained transparent—building trust—with the business leaders. When the team did fall short, they described in detail what could be done to remedy the red items before the end of the next quarter.

3. Keri created an NPS (net promoter score) to find out directly from the leaders if they would recommend the HR team to their colleagues. Keri collected the results and again, in the name of building trust, she shared the results with all business groups. Full transparency. She created an action plan for any score that was less than a 100 percent endorsement, to hold her team accountable.

The key takeaway from this example is that Warriors may strategize, but then they act. The importance of being goal-oriented shows up clearly when it comes to acting on business

Warriors may strategize, but then **they act.**

goals. Warriors don't just understand business goals; they put them into action and get results.

If you want to be a goal-oriented HR Warrior:

- Ask leadership questions. Ask questions every chance you get when you have the CEO, CFO, CIO, or CMO in front of you (or for some of us, the next-level-down managers). Be respectful of their time, of course, but know that it takes only a few minutes to ask one insightful question and learn a little bit more about the business. This method works two ways: you learn about the company and the leadership learns about you. It's win-win.

- Study company materials. Read the white papers, press releases, company blogs, and PR materials. Read what the sales and marketing departments share with clients. Read what local and national news outlets write about your organization. Read the internal documents that HR often have access to but are not made available to the public. You know those PowerPoint presentations that the VP of HR likes to cascade through the department? Read them. There's a reason she is sending them to the entire department. Dedicate twenty or thirty minutes each week to read these materials. Do this when you need a mental break from your work, or the last thirty minutes of your Friday afternoon, when your head feels like a mushy banana. The more you read, the more you know!

- Ask your manager for information. Set up a morning coffee or lunch meeting (or with other HR managers) and ask questions about the "bigger picture" of HR. Find out what are the highest-priority projects that HR is managing, or the upcoming projects, or the plans for the coming year. Ask what are the biggest challenges for HR and the greatest opportunities, and what impact these have on the organization. Pain points the department is feeling? Ask, ask, and then ask some more.

- Dig deep. Remember the "whys" of the quality of accuracy (page 89)? Find out the why behind the why, and the why behind *that* why. Act like a dog looking for his bone. Dig a little deeper!

- Be curious. If you don't know what a term means, ask for clarification. If you don't know why the HR function is focusing so much of its third quarter on compensation analysis, ask. If you aren't making a connection to the company and your job, find out why not. Don't be afraid to be vulnerable.

Being Goal-Oriented in the Workplace

How do you know when you are performing well when it comes to being goal-oriented? When—

- Business leaders say, "You get it!" Listen for affirmation from others that you do understand the business goals.

- Business partners come to you with a problem because they know you will understand the pain point. They ask for your opinions proactively. They demand that you participate in meetings, and ask for your opinions in those meetings. Many leaders consistently hold team meetings and deliberately leave HR off the invite, so these invitations are by no means trivial. Get in there!

- You are not merely a sounding board but are counted on to be a problem solver. You never look for the simple fix but instead identify the root cause of every issue, perform a needs assessment, and dig to find a solution.

- You tie HR metrics to business metrics. This means you can prove your ROI. When HR is measured, it should be measured in the context of the company's goals. You consistently tie the two together. Occasionally, there can be a struggle to identify the hard metrics of HR work (such as how engagement is truly measured), but at a minimum you will have the anecdotes to back up your work. Tell a story to show the results.

- You influence leaders to think differently. After partnering with them, you recognize a demonstrated change in behavior. (No need to rub it in. The "I told you so" approach is not how we demonstrate Warrior status. Please move along to your next partner and repeat the process.)

If a would-be Warrior has not developed the quality of being goal-oriented, things may look like this:

- HR is rarely invited to any functional or leadership meetings.

- HR gets the silent treatment from leaders and business partners. They also get news about organizational changes secondhand.

- Programs initiated by HR die on the vine. They have no traction and garner no support from leadership, or may be defunded by the company because of a lack of clarity about the program's purpose or because of its lack of results.

- When HR projects are halted, defunded, or put on ice, there is little self-assessment as to why this occurred. If a project's goals are clearly stated to the organization—and tied directly to the organization's business goals—they should carry on. If they don't, HR needs to ask why not.

Please know this: we have experienced all these situations. We are not throwing stones (or shade) your way. We recognize these warning signs because we've seen them ourselves; we've failed, we've made mistakes, and we've changed course. Remember, the importance of humility, and don't worry about perfection. Learn from your mistakes and move on quickly. Self-development requires a constant state of change.

A Recap

Many of us have repeated the "Don't just talk the talk, walk the walk" in some form or fashion. Get stuff done! There is a time for talking, and a clear time for action, and the HR Warrior quickly transitions from *knowing* to *doing*. This is a surefire way to gain the trust of our business partners. Many of us know what the opposite looks like: those who have great chops but not great crops. If you are going to invest the time to plant the CHARGE seeds, produce a harvest! Be patient. Learn to love the process of development and continue learning about your company. It will pay off in ways you can't yet imagine. Where being goal-oriented is concerned, the key takeaways are:

- The company's goals are the Warrior's goals. Be keenly aware of what the company wants to accomplish, and align your professional goals with them. This will pay off in career-advancement opportunities.

Learn to love the process of development and continue learning about your company. **It will pay off in ways you can't yet imagine.**

- It's worth it to make the effort to learn. A summary of the company's goals won't arrive in your inbox. Reach out to people and look for resources to find out what these goals are. The more you seek them out, the more you will learn (and the more others will take notice of the role HR is playing).

- Taking strategic action is important. HR should align its work with the business goals. Only when you have thoughtful, specific, and meaningful goals can you deliver the most impact possible on the employees who make the company function.

- Emotions, in all forms, exist everywhere in the workplace, in every form. Warriors strike the balance between understanding the emotions of others and acting with business goals in mind first. This takes practice.

The Check-In

Maintaining focus to achieve any goal is difficult. Whether personal or career-related, distractions exist seemingly everywhere, keeping you from achieving your goals. To be a Warrior means to put aside distraction. Have you ever heard someone say "There are a lot of reasons not to try something, but you only need one reason to go for it"? Believe it! Ask yourself how you display the Warrior quality of being goal-oriented in your daily work by reflecting on the following:

- In your career, what is your most important personal goal?

- Name one goal of the HR Department.

- Name one of the most important company goals.

- Are the three you named above all tied together? If not, consider whether you want to adjust your focus to align your career goals with your organization's goals.

  Now consider your personal goal from above:

- Name something you can do this year to put extra effort towards accomplishing this goal.

- Name a top distraction you face that is keeping you from achieving this goal.

- Have you shared this goal with your manager? Why or why not?

- Do you have a written action plan for achieving this goal?

Although this chapter identifies many reasons to go after a goal, the HR Warrior needs only one. But remember, goals won't get achieved by themselves. Have a Warrior mentality and create goals, set a plan in place to achieve them, and let nothing—not emotions, not the opinions of others, and not your environment—stop you from achieving progress towards HR Warrior.

CHARGE

CHAPTER 8
E Is for Exemplary

K ERI HAS HAD fulfilling partnerships with many VPs over
the course of her career. Whether they worked in Operations, HR, Sales, or Finance, each partnership presented an opportunity for her to build trust. And trust
goes both ways. If Keri remained transparent in her feedback
to the VP, they felt comfortable doing the same with her. And
this level of comfort was in play when Keri received feedback
on one of her employees—feedback that came as a shock.

A newly hired VP wanted to explore the current state of
her division, one that was not meeting the company's expectations, so she asked Keri and her team to show some love to
the branches. During the "love tour" of a West Coast division,
Keri and several members of her team met with employees in
every branch in the three states for one-on-one conversations.
As always, Keri sought to understand the root cause of the
problem, and then create a strategy to make improvements.

One of her methods for starting a dialogue with branch
managers and individual contributors was to ask about their

view of HR. What was working well and what wasn't? Keri and the team wanted to know how they could help the branch succeed, and for this to happen, the partnership needed to function well. To Keri's surprise, the feedback was not good. There were concerns about an HR employee, and these concerns had been festering in the minds of employees and coming out in their hallway conversations for several months.

Keri had two choices: ignore the feedback and continue the "love tour" for its explicit purpose, or deal with this side issue immediately. She chose the latter. Keri shared the feedback with the VP (build trust through transparency) and promised she would make the situation right.

After several discussions with the manager of this HR employee, Keri concluded that employee in question was not going to be successful in her current role. A change had to be made, and so the employee made a career move outside the organization. Keri reported what had happened to her VP partner and the branches that shared their concerns.

These types of situations are not always easy, and they don't always end quickly. In this instance, it took nearly a year for the termination problem to be completely resolved. The branches were greatly appreciative of the leadership Keri had shown, and the bond between branches thousands of miles away from the office were strengthened. It wasn't easy, but love abounded!

SO FAR, WE'VE LOOKED at six qualities we believe should be embodied by and admired in an HR Warrior. The last quality is to be exemplary. Below we pick apart this adjective and provide a thorough understanding of it in an exemplary (we're clever at times) way.

Sometimes we must face that we are in the wrong. As we've stated from the beginning, we don't have all the answers, and honestly, we hope we never do. Just like you, we are on a constant path of learning. And often this education begins by taking a hard look within. What do you need to change about yourself so that you can change the things around you? It's not enough to say the right things or tell others what the right thing is. Warriors practice what they preach. Setting an example is key to becoming a true HR Warrior. Here's how to do that:

- Demonstrate first before demanding anyone else do the same.

- Maintain integrity in every situation, no matter what. No matter what!

- Be a steward of the company culture, environment, and character.

- Be bold! Warriors do not shortchange any employee on great career experiences, and this includes themselves.

- Accept that you do not know everything, and use passion to find a solution for every problem you encounter.

Keep Your Promises

Human Resources often harp on managers about addressing employee performance. Good or bad, employees need to be coached and managed daily. But HR Warriors must do this as well. A manager does not want to be held accountable for coaching employees if HR doesn't do the same.

Imagine that you are a newly promoted manager whose job is immediately complicated by a fifteen-year employee with quite the gripe. This employee is underperforming to the point that it is a detriment to the team. Others complain. His work isn't completed on time, which has an impact on the team's meeting of their deadlines. And to make matters worse, the employee shows no concern about his underperformance—in fact, he spends over an hour a day online applying for other jobs.

You schedule a meeting with HR. You share your frustrations and ask for advice, since you've never had to address performance issues with an employee before. But you also have another problem: although you appreciate your HR partner, he's got a questionable reputation.

Poor performers. These are the HR generalists who don't respond to emails within twenty-four hours, or show up to meetings on time, or have a solid grasp on the employee handbook when doling out shoddy advice. If you were this manager, would you take your HR partner seriously when he tells you to act immediately and create a performance plan? We didn't think so.

But as an HR Warrior, you're a person of your word. It may appear old-fashioned to do business with a handshake, but it is not old-fashioned to be a person who follows through on their promises.

Did you say you would respond to that employee's benefit question by the end of the day? Do it.

Did you say you would schedule a recurring meeting with the new Finance director to help her through her onboarding plan over the course of her first ninety days? Do it.

Did you say you would edit a PowerPoint presentation by the end of the week for your coworker who is nervous about his upcoming training class? Do it.

Integrity Is All-Encompassing

A big part of what HR does is ensure that everyone else follows the common-sense rules we learned in kindergarten. We ask employees to complete annual compliance courses in which they promise not to leave their laptops unattended in public; to avoid sharing confidential financial information with the neighbor, who also happens to be a stockholder; and to sign documents that promise they will not touch coworkers (ever) or speak in a disparaging way about anyone.

And HR is not above these rules. Warriors are most effective when we show, don't tell. If you coach a manager to establish a better onboarding program for new hires in an attempt to lower attrition of early-career employees, you'd better be sure the onboarding plan used within your team is the crème de la crème. If you are leading a class on value-based leadership qualities, you'd better be sure you have followed through on the multiple concerns team members raised about the star player on your own team.

Holding ourselves accountable is a key ingredient in the ability to act in an exemplary fashion. You may believe yourself to be highly ethical—and want to be considered as such—but being exemplary isn't just about knowing what the ethical move is in any given situation. It's about integrity. Integrity takes "Show, don't tell" a step further.

Having integrity in HR means you lead by example. Leading by example means you have credibility within your organization. And credibility means you are believable. You have "been there, done that," and you can share advice. It means (once again) that you are trustworthy.

One way HR demonstrates a lack of integrity is by coasting in the job. This kind of HR Weenie doesn't put in the effort required to do the work, because often there is no clear-cut, easy approach to completing it. For example, let's say an investigation has certain steps that must be followed to come to a conclusion. But if you choose to interview only three of the five employees involved in order to save a miniscule amount of time, you are not thoroughly addressing every concern and, as a result, you are not doing what is in the best interest of the employees, or the company.

Acting with integrity means having the right priorities. Perhaps you have witnessed fellow HR practitioners receive a concern or complaint from an employee, but since it is ten minutes before clock-out time on a Friday before a long holiday weekend, the complaint is shelved. Leaving work at exactly 5 p.m. so you can be one of the first to arrive for happy hour should not be more important than initiating an employee investigation with accuracy. Warriors have a stewardship mentality and are stewards of the company's greatest assets—its people. Warriors must first do right by them, every single day. It is in this way we are exemplary.

Acting with integrity means having the **right priorities.**

Yet pick a day of the week, and pick a time of day, and unethical behavior is occurring somewhere in some company. Do a quick search on the internet of "fired CEOs" and you'll see that examples abound. Unfortunately, part of the negative perception of HR is that we act only as judge and jury of such behavior (ahem, alleged behavior) but do not ourselves consistently demonstrate true north on the moral compass.

You should not have to hashtag the point that integrity counts in HR. Integrity in HR should be practiced without a second thought and, for that matter, without others noticing. The watercooler talk about the latest CEO or company scandal lasts only for a few hours, but reputations—whosoever it is—tend to be ruined indefinitely. HR Warriors prize their reputation and show employees, leadership, and the organization that exemplary HR professionals with integrity are all the rage—and much more than the topic of a hashtag.

Warriors wear integrity like a well-earned badge. Having integrity takes total commitment and a passion to do what is right at every turn. No shortcuts, no hall pass, no cheating off the other kid's test. It's straight-up hard-core work. But as Warriors demonstrate their commitment to do what is right, when it's right, we show our dedication to the organization—and to the culture in which everyone works.

Be a Steward

"Culture" is a popular term. HR loves (and we mean *loves*) to use the word to describe the place in which we live. The island of culture has plenty of happy coconut clients and palm tree personalities, basking in the perfect sunshine. Well, in our dreams at least. "Culture" is an ambiguous term, difficult to quantify with metrics but inescapable in any workplace.

Leave it to HR to manage another intangible measure of success! Warriors have a unique perspective on a company's culture: we are stewards of great experiences in the workplace. Warriors see the workplace as a blank slate—an opportunity for people to learn, accomplish greatness, and, in turn, help their company succeed. And, quite simply, Warriors understand that a company culture is its people. How people speak, how people feel, how people act, and how people work within the four walls of their workplace.

The greater the emphasis that HR places on improving the employee experience, the stronger a company culture becomes. But building a culture like this is done step by step, one moment at a time. HR Warriors are in the boxing ring of company culture, not sitting in the front row with the sixty-four-ounce plastic cup of soda—because employees are worth the fight. Warriors never shy away from a battle and are not afraid to do things the hard way, if the value to the employee outweighs the effort required.

For example, although it might be easier to send updated job descriptions in a long email message to a group of employees rather than conduct one-on-one conversations with each employee on how their roles will change after a reorganization, this comes at the cost of a personalized, thoughtful approach. A mass email saves you time and energy but sets up a culture of lack of caring. HR Warriors who are exemplary think from the perspective of the individual: If I just received news that my company is changing all the job descriptions and I must change jobs, I would be nervous! How would I want to be told? How would I want to go through this change?

Warriors understand this and think with the heart, along with the head, to come up with a strong solution. Warriors

Warriors see the workplace as a blank slate—**an opportunity for people to learn, accomplish greatness, and help their company succeed.**

work as much as needed to come up with a plan that will make a difficult change less stressful. Most importantly, they do this to show employees that the company they work for respects them.

Make Development a Priority

HR Warriors build a strong culture by valuing their own experiences and development as much as they value the experiences and development of all other employees. Personal development for HR Warriors is just as important as for the employees they work with—another way to practice what you preach.

Our story of the large company transformation offers many examples of Warrior qualities, but is also a good example of taking on one's own development, a key attribute of the exemplary Warrior. Keri's team wanted to be as prepared as possible to be the leaders of the change management project. Knowing how much work and effort was required to accurately build such a large change management plan and deliver it with the company's goals in mind, Keri wanted her team to be educated in key change practices.

She attended an intensive Prosci training program to become a certified change practitioner. Prosci is an organization that's developed a people-first change management practice, one that Keri taught her team. She immediately scheduled a three-day, in-person training class that she would lead, along with time for additional study of the Prosci's change model, ADKAR (an acronym for awareness, desire, knowledge, ability, and reinforcement).

Attending the training class and then doing additional

study was work Keri's staff did on top of their day-to-day responsibilities. Their organization would be going through such a significant change, it was critical they executed it right the first time. There would be no second chances for the leadership, nor for the HR team.

Not only did this additional education benefit the company as it powered through months of change but it gave every HR employee a highlight to add to their résumé. They demonstrated their value to the organization by expanding their knowledge and building expertise. As Keri told her team many times, "The goal of every HR practitioner should be to add something to your résumé every year of your career."

WHEN WARRIORS DEMONSTRATE their level of commitment to their work, employees take notice. Warriors who are invested in doing a thorough job, who read books on their profession, who research key resources in the industry, and who have a passion for improving encourage employees to do the same.

Displaying the qualities of an HR Warrior requires full commitment—and it may involve working overtime. However, it's important to maintain work-life balance and pursue passions, interests, and relationships that help fill up your cup after a long day at the office.

HR practitioners have a natural stewardship mentality, and Warriors are stewards of their own development. They apply for promotional opportunity. They contact the hiring manager to discuss the role before a formal interview. They study and prepare. And they tell themselves, "I am the most qualified candidate for this role." So, go ahead and volunteer for that nonpaying project at work. Don't do it for the money, do it for the development and exposure. Raise your hand and ask to be involved, even if the project is outside of HR or you are uncertain about how to do it. Even if the project adds five hours of work to your weekly schedule.

MONICA WAS WORKING in an entry-level HR job when an opportunity opened up. A high-performing team of HR professionals and talent professionals needed to hire an HR consultant. The director of this team (who happened to be Keri) wanted to open this role to HR first. She spread the word throughout the department: Come join our team and work harder than you ever have in your life!

Such an invitation could either excite or scare off people. Monica was excited. There was just one problem: she didn't meet the qualifications of the role as laid out in the job description, which specified five years of experience in an HR generalist role. Monica had eighteen months of being a semi-generalist, mostly as an assistant. The description also noted that applicants with three years of experience supporting a leader or a division, or equivalent leadership experience, were preferred. Monica had zero. And the "preferred PHR or SPHR certification"? Well, Monica wasn't even sure what those acronyms stood for.

But, at the end of the workday, after receiving the all-HR email about the job opening, Monica crept up to Keri's cubicle and asked if she should apply. Four interviews later, Keri offered Monica the job. Monica's response?

"You know I don't know anything about HR, right?"

Keri said, "Yes, but you can learn that. You have the exact core of what it takes to succeed."

The Pursuit of Excellence

In the movies, a warrior is often depicted as infallible. Someone who cannot lose, cannot be defeated, who plows ahead with stoic bravery into the most insurmountable battles, and wins every time. These superhuman protagonists have superhuman strength. Yes, we want everyone in HR to be a Warrior, but this doesn't mean we must wear suits of steel.

To be exemplary is to be fallible, not bulletproof. The world of HR changes daily, and it is impossible to stay knowledgeable about all the rules and regulations governing Human Resources. Be bold enough to raise a hand even when you don't know the answer. Be smart enough to find the answer. Be strong enough to never quit. Don't shortchange your business partners or yourselves.

Because regulations and laws are passed, rescinded, or modified almost daily and, on top of that, they vary among municipalities, cities, and states, oftentimes the only answer we have for our business partners is "I don't know." But the HR Warrior follows that statement with "But I will find out."

Do you know how many states have implemented "ban the box" legislation? Do you know which states currently ban inquiries into candidates' salary history? Do you know what the minimum wage law is for your state, and how this will increase in the coming years? And then there is California... And what if you have employees in Puerto Rico? Or in Mexico? Or Canada?

The point is this: you do not need to have the answer to all these questions. If you earn a PHR, SPHR, HRCI, or other HR-related certification (yes, we have a lot of abbreviations in HR!), that's great. You can attend SHRM (Society of Human

Resources) or HCI (Human Capital Institute) conferences to stay up-to-date on industry news and information. And there are many outstanding organizations, networking events, and online groups that can help you remain keenly aware of important workplace trends. Self-education is tremendously important for the exemplary Warrior, but the truth is, you will never know everything.

IN THE EARLY DAYS of growing her company, Abbracci Group, Keri signed a contract with one of her first clients, a small firm with a talented leadership team that wanted to build a strong

Self-education is important for the exemplary Warrior, **but the truth is, you will never know everything.**

HR foundation with the ability to scale as the business grew. The firm needed support with many of its HR functions. In one of the first phone calls, in which the firm was still feeling out Abbracci, the executive asked Keri, "With your expertise and varied background, is there anything that you don't provide?"

Keri said, "Compensation and benefits." She was honest, and the potential client appreciated that honesty. Some firms looking to win business would lie—"We can do it all. We know it all. We can fix every problem you have in your company, and it comes at a reasonable fee." But Keri knew the importance of this relationship relied on transparency up front—we don't know compensation, and we don't know benefits. There are experts for that, and they're not us.

Keri's company won their business. Interestingly, one of the major projects for this client was compensation banding. Keri partnered with an outside specialist and implemented a new compensation structure for the client—and learned a huge amount throughout the process.

As a Warrior, you will be asked to do things that you've never done before, because your clients trust you will be committed to solving the problems. Here is what Warriors do when they don't have the answer:

- Research to find the answer.
- Find someone who is an expert and ask for their help.
- Give the problem to an expert to solve.
- Ask the right questions of the expert to learn the answer.

The answer "I don't know" is not a dead end. It's a starting point. Exemplary means that when you don't have an answer, you look for one. Consider all the resources that exist today.

We have no shortage of people who broadcast that they are an expert in any given subject. Human Resources encompasses many aspects of the workplace—from culture to employee engagement to talent development to benefits to recruiting—and you can't expect to know it all. But you can pursue knowledge and make a commitment to tackle any problem.

Exemplary in the Workplace

Exemplary behavior does not require perfection, but you can get close to it during your pursuit of knowledge and excellence. Let's look at examples of exemplary Warrior behavior in the workplace:

- Warriors show first, talk second. They act with excellence and then coach others on how to do the same.

- Warriors put in extra effort. They arrive early, stay late, and volunteer for work-related projects, without being asked to.

- Warriors have examples to share with managers and other employees who are struggling. "Been there, done that" is their approach, and it works.

- Warriors expect excellence from their HR teams before they expect it from their business partners.

- Warriors have a passion for a strong and vibrant company culture, and they demonstrate this through their commitment to the company goals and their respect for its employees.

- Warriors seek out growth opportunities for themselves.

- Warriors seek out growth opportunities for other employees.

- Warriors boldly raise their hand for assignments that are a stretch. They seek to add to their résumé every year.

- Warriors admit when they don't have the answer.

- Warriors search for a solution to every problem.

- Warriors seek out experts for help.

And here are examples of the opposite end of the spectrum. They may seem familiar to you if you've worked with anyone in HR who lacks the exemplary quality:

- An HR manager coaches a business leader on giving timely and relevant feedback to an underperformer. Yet that same HR manager has had an underperforming employee on their team for three years, with complaints from business partners, yet no changes have been made.

- An HR employee investigates an employee for transferring sensitive information in an insecure manner but overlooks their team's practice of sharing "stories" with the rest of the department via email.

- An HR leader doesn't meet with their new hire but counsels multiple business leaders on the importance of following the six-month onboarding plan.

- An HR director chides business leaders for going over their budget, when their own department is padded with too many generalists, resulting in a high headcount.

- A generalist who does not pick up the phone when it rings at 5:03 p.m., but grabs her coat from the back of her chair and leaves for the day.

- A performance consultant copies the same development plan for every employee on the sales operations team—why bother creating something different for each person?

- An HR team places the company webinar on mute so they can online chat with each other about the destination options for happy hour.

- An HR manager assumes that a group of employees are exempt (i.e., salaried) because researching FLSA (Fair Labor Standards Act) guidelines on the difference between exempt and nonexempt statuses would take too long.

As we've said, HR is being watched, and Warriors know this. People want to see what the "integrity police" do, and often take cues from your behavior as to what they can get away with. We do not condone this approach, but we do condone the "Do as I say and as I do" approach. Set the example for what exemplary behavior looks like each day. Personal growth is a huge commitment—and an exciting opportunity!

A Recap

Whew! We covered a lot in this chapter. But being thorough is exactly what it takes to be exemplary. Being exemplary takes no less time than developing courage, humility, accuracy, resilience, or goal-orientation. It's the maraschino cherry on top of the sundae. It's the ribbon ready to be ripped through at the finish line. It's the end-of-quarter bonus for surpassing expectations. Exemplary is not enough, it's being more than enough! Warriors are not the median, the average, or the "pass" in a pass-or-fail test. Warriors aim for greatness.

Recall how we defined an HR Warrior in Chapter 1:

The HR Warrior is a professional who can be counted on to get the job done right, to exceed expectations, to inspire others, and to set the expectations that increase the work output of everyone around them. HR Warriors care about what they do. They see their work as an opportunity to have a positive impact on the business every day.

And don't forget to enjoy the process, because the Warrior qualities we have described throughout this book take time to develop. Here are the key takeaways from this chapter:

- An exemplary HR Warrior demonstrates the right behaviors first, before asking others to do the same. Be a leader who sets the standard.

- Integrity is critical if you want the reputation of reliability and credibility in the workplace. Do not underestimate the importance of integrity.

- The HR Warrior is a steward of the company culture, environment, and character.

- The HR Warrior has a passion for improving at their job. They are as passionate about their own career growth as about that of the employees they work for.

- The HR Warrior is willing to be honest and admit that they don't know everything—but will work hard to find the answer.

The Check-In

It's important to be able to step back and provide an accurate assessment of your workplace. And for those in HR, it's especially important to understand your role in shaping that environment—not only for yourself but also for those you work with. Consider the last coaching conversation you had (whether it was with a manager, another employee, or even a friend):

- Was this conversation an opportunity to share wisdom with someone and help them in the process?

- How did this person respond to your feedback? Did they agree or disagree with it?

- In your coaching, did you provide examples from your own experiences to show that you've "been there, done that"?

Let's say that a friend wants to apply for a job at your company. How would you answer these questions?

- How would you describe your company's culture?

- What is your role, in HR, on influencing that culture?

- What development opportunities exist for you?

- How have you grown in your job since you joined the company?

- Would you recommend that your friend work at the company?

CHAPTER 9

CHARGE Your Way to Success

AYBE, AFTER READING about the six essential qualities of an HR Warrior, you said to yourself, "This is nothing more than common sense!" But while in theory it may sound easy to implement these fundamentals, in practice, it's far more complex. Remember the tools we provided in Chapter 2, the HR Weenie-to-Warrior Assessment and the Organizational Assessment? In part, they showed that you cannot develop into an HR Warrior in a vacuum. How you function in your job day to day can be significantly impacted by the environment in which you work.

In this chapter, we share ideas of what to do if your work environment hinders your ability to become an HR Warrior. Our advice is not like the latest crash diet, on which you drop fifteen pounds before your cousin's wedding next weekend. These recommendations are for enduring and simple ways to view your career and take control of your growth plan.

Some of you may feel like you are already exhibiting many of the HR Warrior qualities, and that you work in a safe, respectable environment that allows you to flourish. We are nothing but happy for you! (On an unrelated note, please send us an email with the name of your employer.) But if you are like the many employees out there who struggle with some level of discomfort or disengagement within their organization, we want to help.

But let us be clear: we want to help *you*; we are not here to pass judgment on your company. This book is about taking action, taking control, and managing the sticky, messy, emotional process along the way. We are not here to give you one-liners to picket in front of your company's front doors. Every company is different, every company faces business challenges, and every company has a different culture, a different philosophy, and different guiding principles.

The Way of the HR Warrior allows you to define your path to success, and as you march along that path, to encourage and inspire those around you. You can change your company from the inside out!

"But my company doesn't value HR" we hear many of you say. (That is how we defined an "HR Problem" in the Organizational Assessment.) That's okay. Well, actually, it's not okay. Let us explain. Inside every challenge lies opportunity. If your company demonstrates a lack of support for the HR function, that presents a huge opportunity for you to make a difference. An opportunity for you to change the hearts and minds of those around you. And an opportunity to transform the brand of HR.

That sounds like a lot of work, and it is. But all you need to focus on is what's within your control. What can you do today to make a difference?

The Way of the Warrior Is to Have (and Manage) Emotions

It's easy to give up when the times get tough. But it's in those tough moments that you find out whether you really want to achieve a goal. When things are not going according to plan, that's the time you need perseverance. And part of persevering is recognizing that emotions will run high.

Emotions will surface when you hear that the HR Department will soon face layoffs; when you learn that the training program you spent three months planning will be slashed because of corporate budget cuts; and when your manager, who has been a mentor to you, unexpectedly resigns. The workplace is not devoid of emotion, especially when you work alongside people you see more often than your family

When things are not going according to plan, that's the time you need **perseverance.**

and friends. You must be tough to get through the low days in order to experience the high days. Especially when the low days outnumber the high days.

In these trying moments, allow yourself to step away from the battlefield. Get out of the building and take a walk during your lunch break. Cry a few tears if you need to. Head to your local gym after work to take a yoga or kickboxing class. Schedule a meeting with a mentor or someone who encourages you. Take thirty minutes to read a few inspiring articles on topics you are passionate about. Schedule a day off from work and take your dog to a park. Find a way to fill your fuel tank back up! Just know that you are in growth mode. And growth mode can feel painful. Just like when you help a family member move into their new house and insist that you are strong enough to lift the solid-wood end tables but the next day regret your actions. You are sore. You did something unusual and difficult, and your body reminds you of this for days to come. It's the same way with emotions. They show up powerfully when we are going through something difficult, uncomfortable, exciting, new, or scary, and this includes those times when we are simultaneously struggling and learning.

In Chapter 2's "Overall Picture" chart (page 39), "study" is shown as being at the intersection between an HR Weenie and an organization that is either a Promoter or a Potential partner, and "growth" is shown as being at the intersection of HR Wishful and an organization that is a Potential partner. If this is where you find yourself, you are showing signs of a perspective and a willingness to develop into an HR Warrior, and your organization is showing signs of valuing and utilizing HR in a meaningful way. This can be a tremendously positive place to be. But taking advantage of this position will require you to be brave.

We talked about how to take chances to grow as an HR professional in Chapter 3, on courage, and asked you to think about ways to take courageous actions at work. This could mean doing something that scares you, like joining Toastmasters and speaking in front of a group of strangers, or asking for that promotion you've been wanting for the past six months. It also means giving direct and honest feedback to leadership, at the risk of them not responding to it well.

We ourselves seized a growth opportunity by writing this book. The process of collecting the ideas, successes, challenges, and feedback of business leaders and HR professionals into this book was a way for us to develop new skills and connect with many other professionals.

When Keri wanted to start a company "someday," Monica asked her, "Why not do it in six months?" Although at the time, Keri thought that was a little crazy, but those words encouraged her to think big. Since she started her own company, every day brings Keri a new challenge—business development, creating and adjusting solutions based on client feedback, forming new partnerships, and networking—and a little bit of fear. Now, that is one big growth opportunity!

Stretching yourself doesn't need to be as dramatic as starting your own company; it can be finding ways to work with a difficult manager. Or signing up for a local networking event to meet like-minded professionals. Grow, grow, grow!

The Way of the Warrior Is to Overcome Resistance

It would be great if you could set goals one day and achieve them the next. If you want to run a half-marathon, think how fantastic it would be if this was accomplished after one sweaty workout! The world would be full of fit, healthy, supercharged athletes. The personal training industry and self-help publishing on how to live a healthier lifestyle would take a big hit. Who needs guidance if your body can change overnight?

As much as you might wish you could set goals one day and achieve them the next, there would be a dangerous side effect if that were actually the case. Personal willpower would be nonexistent, and you would not need to build up any amount of discipline or diligence. The joy of overcoming struggles, and the victory, would not taste as sweet. You would miss out on building camaraderie with teammates and helping others achieve their goals. No pep talks, no cheerleading, no motivational speeches, no discipline.

That sounds rather boring.

But if you allow yourself to grow over time, the victory does taste much sweeter. When you take ownership over your goals and show a willingness to stay the course over time, you grow significantly as a person. Habits need time to develop, and you build habits in your life when you are working towards accomplishing your goals.

The same goes for organizations. It takes time to see a company change its culture and its environment. But little by little, changes occur. The first time you meet with a front-line manager and he isn't responsive to your speech about the importance of having an onboarding plan for new employees, don't give up. Find a way to show him.

The next time you meet a new hire on her first day on the job, set up an appointment for the following week, a quick ten-minute meeting to find out how the first week went. Did she get all her questions answered? Does she know the lay of the land? Has she completed her new-hire training courses?

Don't give up. **Be patient.** Solutions don't always crop up overnight.

What does she need, and how can you help her? The answers to these questions will be helpful feedback to a manager who is resistant to your onboarding recommendations.

Repeat this process thirty or sixty days later. Take five minutes to talk to the new employee and gather firsthand intel about how the job is going, and her experiences as a new employee. This is incredibly important information. It is honest information that should be shared with the manager.

Summarize the employee's feedback for the manager. What trends are you seeing, what issues come up, what does the new hire need? Then explain how a thorough onboarding plan can fix any of the gaps for this employee. Ta-da!

Small actions over an extended period will lead to results, no matter how small. The manager may now understand the importance of an onboarding plan. Even if he still resists implementing such a program (the shop floor is just too busy for such a process, he may say), you still gathered useful data on the employee experience for him. Don't give up. Be patient; solutions don't always crop up overnight. And who knows, this manager may just surprise you and change his mind about implementing the onboarding plan.

This scenario is an example of the "frustration" mode, as seen in the "Overall Picture" chart in Chapter 2. In this book, we discuss how some business leaders do not find value in HR (again, that would be an "HR Problem" organization, according to our Organizational Assessment, page 34), but regardless of what others think, you still have the potential to become a Warrior, even in that kind of organization.

Sometimes leaders make decisions that you have very little control over but which have a significant impact on you. What if the CEO wants to cut the HR budget? Keep your emotions in check and don't throw the doors open at the next leadership summit and demand that the CEO change their mind. We also do not recommend that you take to social media to criticize this decision. We do recommend creating a plan—a plan of action for what you can control in an uncontrollable situation. Here are a few examples of what we mean.

Some decisions are significant within any company. It can come as a shock when the CEO or head of HR announces there will be budget cuts within the department. Then the head of HR announces a department-wide restructure of roles and rewrite of job duties. Another shock! And when the company leadership wants to outsource some of HR's work? What can you do about it? Here are a few ideas of how to take a situation that is out of your control and bring it back under your control:

- Schedule a meeting with your manager to determine the level of impact to employees.

- Create a list of ways you can make yourself more valuable to your current employer.

- Find out if any critical roles are currently vacant within HR and consider whether you want to apply for these roles.

Don't give up on your career or on your personal development just because leadership makes big decisions that affect HR.

What if it's business as usual in the HR Department, yet the company has a culture that doesn't value HR? For example, the HR team is relegated to process payroll, update the employee handbook, post job descriptions for open roles, interview candidates, and complete the termination paperwork. That is the value-add that the company you work for sees in HR. But you want to do so much more! You believe you have so much more value to add. What do you do? Here are a few suggestions:

- Identify two to three actions you could take in the current year to elevate your level of work.

- Share your ideas with your manager and ask for permission to implement them. (Without adding any cost to the company or taking away from your current responsibilities.)

- Create a list of questions you can bring with you when you meet with your business partners. These questions can help you determine what their needs are and identify ways you can help.

- Act on the needs of your business partners. Share with them a plan of how you can help them, with goals, action items, due dates, and dates when you will provide progress updates.

- Ask for feedback from business partners on the services you currently provide. Determine whether there is a gap between what you are doing and what they want you to do.

- Continue learning. Read books, articles, and other resources to grow personally and professionally. Network with other professionals.

- Share your results with HR leadership. Demonstrate the great work you can provide to your business partners.

What if you've tried some or all of these approaches, but the leadership still doesn't give you permission to take on more strategic HR work? What if you feel stifled in your role, and you don't have the support of your manager?

Consider leaving your company.

We don't say this lightly. Changing jobs is a significant life event. There is always a level of risk when you accept a new job—will it truly be better, will this manager be any different, will the company culture be what it says it is? Even with the risk factors, it is sometimes necessary to leave our current environment in search of something better. There is a way to respectfully handle this process.

Be sure you have tried everything. Have you conducted several conversations with your manager and HR leadership to determine whether your current responsibilities can change? Evaluate if you've made any progress with business partners or HR partners to advance the HR Warrior cause. Determine whether your skills and abilities could be more effectively put to use if you held a different role in the HR Department.

And meanwhile, continue to network. Make connections with those in professional groups, and keep your eyes and ears open for other opportunities. Update your résumé, and review job postings; consider applying.

If it really is time for you to leave, do so with the utmost professionalism. Provide your employer with advance notice and show up for work every day through to your final day. Don't shortchange your employer just because you want to start your new role. Demonstrate exemplary behavior throughout your final weeks. Transition incomplete work to someone else, and do so with complete honesty. Say goodbye to your business partners and coworkers (especially those you have maintained a strong relationship with). Don't burn any bridges, because you never know when you may come across those people in the HR community, or elsewhere.

HR Warriors have set high standards for themselves, and by doing so, they help create high standards for those around them.

The Way of the Warrior Raises Expectations

You've heard the phrase "Do as I say, not as I do"? That is not how an HR Warrior works. Warriors don't need to say anything. Even in the most uncomfortable situations (like resigning from your job), an HR Warrior handles things like a pro. Exemplary behavior leaves a lasting impression.

HR Warriors ask others to "do as I do." Actions speak loudly. If you are partnering with someone in the business who couldn't care less about your opinions on a messy employee relations issue, do not stampede out of the room, slamming the door hard so as to make a statement. Confidently take a moment and share the reason your feedback is important.

Encourage the manager to fight through a knee-jerk response to terminate the employment, but instead, share the implications of firing an employee when that employee does not have any documented coaching or performance issues.

Expect more from that manager, without telling them "I expect more out of you." (That parenting technique will not get you very far.) Instead, lead by example. Follow up with the manager. Continue to encourage them to take fifteen minutes to document their concerns about the employee. Encourage them to meet with the employee one-on-one and confidentially share this feedback on performance. Volunteer to sit in on this meeting if the manager is uncomfortable leading the conversation. Encourage them to follow through on the agreed-upon steps.

Encouragement can do a lot to build others' confidence. And Warriors want to build the confidence of those who work around them. If your fellow HR coworkers are not HR Warriors (but more like HR Weenies), the temptation can be to let them know this. Or to keep your distance.

But HR Warriors raise the bar for everyone by first raising the bar for themselves. Share what projects you are working on and the excellent results you are seeing at the next HR meeting. Take a coworker to lunch and find out how their job is going. What is going well, and what are they struggling with? Do you have relatable experiences that could help them? Provide updates to your manager about the great feedback you've received from business partners and clients. Share the book or article you read with others in HR so that they too can learn from it.

It's easy to keep the focus on ourselves. But the "selfie" life is not the HR Warrior way. As you develop high expectations for yourself, encourage others to do the same. This is how a

No one works alone. You can accomplish more with others than you can on your own.

team of HR Warriors is formed. No one works alone. You can accomplish more with others than you can on your own.

The Way of the Warrior Involves Reaching Out for Help

Have you ever heard someone say that the only constant is change? That's certainly true when it comes to learning. Learning is a continual process. Learning never ends. The very act of learning means we are getting better. Warriors love the process of learning, but even more, Warriors love the process of learning from others.

Take advantage of the resources at your company, and this includes the people you work with. Sometimes it can feel like you should read books by world-renowned scholars or by those who have the most abbreviations behind their surname. These resources are helpful. But don't forget about your coworkers. You are surrounded by a lot of smart people almost every day!

If you have a new project that involves a lot of change management principles, talk to someone who has worked in a project management office. Talk to someone who has earned their Project Management Professional (PMP) certification. Get advice on how you can manage your project better. If you are now responsible for helping develop a commission structure for a newly created sales role, talk to someone in compensation. Talk to a manager who has designed such plans before for their own teams. If you want to know how to speak more effectively in front of an audience because you are leading a training class in the coming months, talk to someone who is already excellent at it. Did you attend a company meeting where the speaker impressed you? Ask them to lunch and find out their tips and tricks.

You are surrounded by knowledgeable people, and when you are on the way to becoming a Warrior, you learn from others. You are humble enough to understand that learning is a continual state, and there is much to be learned from what others have experienced. A wise phrase to remember is "Don't be the smartest person in the room."

We grow the most when we surround ourselves with people who are smarter, more talented, and more successful than we are. Just like we can help the people we work with raise their expectations of themselves, we can raise our expectations of ourselves by being around talented people. Learning is a two-way street.

Don't only take advantage of opportunities to learn from people in your workplace; take advantage of the many, many resources that exist today to help you grow as an HR Warrior:

- Identify the most-read blogs, websites, and e-newsletters in the HR industry and read them. Create a recurring calendar invitation for when you want to take a dedicated amount of time each week (or month) to read the latest posted material.

- Research well-known books on the profession, on management and leadership, on companies. This includes autobiographies, biographies, nonfiction, and educational books. Make a list of which books you want to read that year, and challenge yourself to stick to your goal. Then repeat the next year.

- Find business leaders and industry experts to follow on social media. But don't just click the button to "follow." They have taken the time to post information—read it! Instead of searching only for what your friends are doing, see what business professionals are doing.

- Attend conferences and business networking events. Introduce yourself to others, swap business cards, send follow-up emails to stay in contact with people you've met. Use events not only as an opportunity to learn what's new in the industry but to meet like-minded professionals. And if networking terrifies you, read one of the many good books out there that teach introverts how to successfully network. No more excuses!

Being a part of a community helps build your confidence. It helps you in times of need (when you need someone else's expertise), but it also helps you give back—by finding ways to advance the cause of the HR Warrior, by encouraging and uplifting others, and by caring about the HR industry more than about the paycheck you receive. The more we advance the profession, the greater the number of HR Warriors out there.

We want everyone to find the intersection between the HR Warrior and the HR Promoter organization. Second best is an HR Wishful who works for a company that has the Potential to become that exceptional Promoter! Warriors are always in high demand. Ask yourself: By advancing my career, how can I help others? And just as important, how can I help my company by giving it all I have to offer?

The HR Warrior community is here to help its members. Join us! Visit our website (www.warriorsofhr.com) to find a list of resources to jump-start development ideas for yourself.

CHAPTER 10

Keri and Monica in Conversation

T HE INSPIRATION TO WRITE a book for HR professionals grew organically from our collective experiences, conversations, and storytelling in the days when we worked together. Here are some of our thoughts on the process, our hope for the book, and what's next.

Why did you want to write this book?

MONICA: Keri brought the idea to me. We were working together at a company, and she talked about how passionate she was to see HR transform and gain the respect it deserves. She knew I liked to write, and I knew she had the perfect way of showcasing what HR can do. She had the respect of a lot of business leaders. She did things differently, and I thought to myself, "We've really got something here." The research we did on what HR books have been published and are still in print showed us that our concept for a book—a practical, brutally honest (and, okay, a bit sassy) approach to why HR has a bad rap and how we can help change that—filled a void.

A lot of books take an academic, research-heavy approach to explaining how to execute the HR business model, and how to excel at executing certain aspects of the Human Resources job. But we didn't find any books that told it to readers straight. We wanted to be the ones to do it.

KERI: Throughout my career, I have witnessed a disturbing lack of basic HR skills. And when I have seen successful HR professionals, they have the fundamentals that we talk about in this book. They are as passionate as I am about Human Resources. And I am equally passionate to see more CHARGE professionals in companies all over the world. As Monica and I brainstormed our book idea, we came across many competency models and strategic theories. But what we felt was lacking was a book that talked about the fundamentals—what skills do you need to have before you move on to the strategic theories?

As we defined the fundamentals, our model saw numerous iterations—it went through the development like we talk about in the book. With our collective experiences and the PhD I earned, I felt that Monica and I could write an insightful book and give the HR profession a major boost. We are tired of the bad rap that HR professionals have!

What do you hope readers will take away from this book?
MONICA: I hope readers will be motivated to act. That may sound trite, but it's true. As soon as I started working in HR, I realized that I was not the cool kid at the lunchroom table. To be honest, I couldn't understand why. The people I was working with were some of the most talented and intelligent

and hardworking people I knew professionally, so the fact that others in the company didn't see HR the same way as I did shocked me. That is when I realized HR had an unfortunate problem. I grew to love the HR function, whereas most people around me don't love it.

I am hopeful that readers will be motivated by understanding that we have control over what happens with HR for years to come. And by developing the CHARGE qualities, we not only can have a big impact on the course of our careers but can set new standards in the companies we work.

KERI: Don't doubt that you can be an HR Warrior! Keep fighting the good fight, because HR Warriors are needed. Find people who support you in your development. Life is too short to be surrounded by negativity and unnecessary drama.

My second hope is that readers will laugh. If you don't have a sense of humor, then you shouldn't work in HR. Sometimes my humor can be dark, I admit. Just because we laugh about things doesn't mean we don't care. It means we need moments in which to let off steam, because this can be a tough job. For me, humor alleviates the tension in tough situations and allows our business and HR partners to laugh about those tough circumstances.

Third, I hope that readers find practical help in this book and feel the love from fellow HR practitioners. We wrote this book from a caring place, and it's about making it work *for you*. We want HR Warriors in every company all over the world. I am a hippie at heart, and I want there to be peace and love in the world, and I want to be a part of that change. HR is where I have the influence to see change happen, but I also know that it's not all about the theoretical. Our roles come down to implementation. And implementation is often the most difficult part of our jobs. We can say that HR should be strategic, but how do we get there? That's what this book is about.

Who were your HR coaches?

MONICA: Keri! That's why I was so excited when she asked me to write a book with her. I remember applying for an open HR consultant role on her team—I knew it was a long shot. I didn't meet the minimum experiences listed on the job description, but I thought, "Why not, lean in!" I applied and made it through multiple interviews with other HR leaders. To my surprise, Keri offered me the job. I remember my exact words in response: "You know I don't know anything about HR, right?" I can be a little too honest at times. She said she knew that, but that she knew I could do it—I had the fundamentals, and the rest of the job I could learn. That was the confidence boost I needed to launch my HR career.

My second most influential coach was my first HR manager, who taught me all those things that I didn't know once I started in the job. And I was fortunate enough to have him as my manager twice in my career. He didn't teach me about employment laws or about compensation charts, but he did teach me how to overcome objections. How to talk persuasively with managers. How to understand the business goals and lead with those goals in one-on-one conversations. This is when I grew most as an HR Warrior.

KERI: I wish I could tell you that I had the most amazing HR mentors and leaders. But what I often learned from observing those in leadership was what *not* to do: laying off employees in a disrespectful way, not coaching for strong employees, and keeping employees from feeling welcome to share their

thoughts openly. And unfortunately, I learned that not everyone on your team has the right motivations for the actions
they take. And this can be painful. What I've told my teams
over the years is that sometimes you can learn more from poor
managers than you can from good managers. But either way,
never stop learning.

I have worked with amazing team members. Some of my
direct reports have challenged me to think outside the box,
and the mix of experiences, personalities, and strengths on my
teams have made me a more well-rounded Warrior. Becoming a people leader stretched me in significant ways, and I've
always wanted various people with opinions, skills, and back-
grounds on my team. This is how we are stronger: together.

My business partners have taught me how HR is perceived,
which is why I knew we had a big problem when it came to our
reputation as a profession. They showed me how to view the
business through a lens different from my own, and what it
means to have a voice and share my perspective when making
business decisions.

Why do you love HR?

MONICA: Because I like to work with people! I like the conflu-
ence of the job: how we can take the employee's perspective,
and the company's perspective, and find creative solutions
to complex problems so that both groups are happy. I like the
challenge of dealing with people—their unpredictability. You
never quite know what's going to happen any given day, and
we have plenty of stories to prove that point. And when the
unexpected happens, I love figuring out how to manage the
emotions and find solutions.

KERI: Like I said, I'm a hippie at heart. With my educational background in psychology, I never thought I would work in HR, but the practical side of me won: I needed to make money! After earning advanced degrees in global HR, peace, and conflict resolution, and human development and organizational systems, I had a huge amount of debt. Going into the corporate sector seemed like an unlikely career path at first. But I quickly realized that the most influential department on the lives of employees is HR. It's possible to make a positive difference, and we get to be ringside for all the people drama (we are not in the balcony, eating popcorn). Plus, I enjoy fighting for the underdogs. For those who feel disenchanted, those who are poorly treated, or those who aren't thought of as smart enough—I want to fight for those employees.

Now that you've coauthored this book, what's next for you?

MONICA: The next book! I don't think either of us feel that we've said everything yet. And we are excited to start conversations with readers, to understand what else is going on with regard to HR. What challenges are others facing that we didn't address in this book? And what do business leaders have to say about HR? I could see us writing another book directed at business leaders: what to expect from your HR team, how to hire HR Warriors, how to utilize HR Warriors, and so on. This book focuses on HR professionals. But let's not forget that it takes two to tango—that HR professionals work with leaders.

KERI: Great question—I have no idea! I have many long-term goals, and as soon as I am on track with my plans, things change. My strategy is this: If I can look back at the last year and say "Great, I grew!," I'm on the right track. If I can look back and say "Damn, I accomplished that?," even better! I can remember only one year of my life where I couldn't say either, and there were quite a few tears over that.

What we want to do is hear from readers. What ideas do they have to CHARGE to the next level? Workshops? Another book? Monthly chats? Personalized coaching? We will listen to what you have to say.

And lastly, my passion is seeing companies transform for the better, and helping employees develop. That I will always be working on.

In what ways do you think HR will change in the next ten years?

MONICA: From my vantage point, it seems that HR will continue to expand its role in influencing the strategic direction of the company when it comes to talent. Everyone is fighting for the best talent and fighting to keep the best talent. And although HR has been a part of these conversations for a long time, I see HR taking the next steps and leading the conversations. Bringing ideas and solutions to the leadership team, rather than the other way around. I see HR being asked to help fix talent problems, and with a greater level of trust that they can act more autonomously than we have experienced in the past.

KERI: If we knew for certain what the future holds, we would create the best products and experience a lot of success! All kidding aside, I do think HR will continue to evolve into a more personalized function as we seek to understand the needs of individual employees. The challenges we face in HR will become more complex, such as how to interpret data collected through precise analytics, how to create programs to develop global leaders, how to integrate AI into the workforce, and how to better manage virtual teams. These will be big challenges, and this requires a lot of HR Warriors!

Tell us about one of the craziest things you've experienced working in HR.

MONICA: That's a difficult one, because it's difficult to pick just one. But without breaking any confidentiality or getting myself into legal trouble, I can tell you several examples. For instance, everyone wants a pay increase. I don't think any of us feel that we are paid what we deem ourselves being worth. A few particular employees come to mind: an hourly employee working twelve-hour shifts, a soon-to-be-mom who wanted to further her career, and a manager who felt he was finally ready for the promotion. I encouraged all these employees to ask for a pay increase. The crazy part is how their managers were resistant to the employees speaking up for themselves. This doesn't happen every day, but it did happen in these circumstances. And having that honest conversation in which you make the case for an employee is difficult but worthwhile. Sometimes all people need is someone to believe in them or to encourage them to do something daring.

KERI: This is an interesting one, and there are countless stories I would like to share, many of them sex related! The number of times we had to deal with employees who commit inappropriate acts at work is astounding. And let's just say that, shockingly, more than once did we have an employee relations issue dealing with people's—ahem—bodily functions, both in and outside the bathroom. Let's just leave it there.

As an HR Warrior, what is in your development plan?

MONICA: Pursuing networking opportunities. It can be very tempting to do our job, go home at the end of the day, and settle into home life. This isn't necessarily a bad thing—we all have family and friends, but what's also important is that we build our professional network. We learn from each other, and we find opportunities to learn when we surround ourselves with smart people. I plan to make a concerted effort to attend networking events and introduce myself to successful professionals.

KERI: Patience. I am not a very patient person, and I don't suffer fools gladly. I make quick decisions, and I want everything done right the first time. But I've seen enough to know that this does not always happen, whether on my team, with my business partners, or with leadership. Sometimes all I need to do is take a breath. Slow down and not taking action is sometimes the best decision I can make.

Keri, you started your own company. Why the name "Abbracci Group"?

KERI: The name wasn't our first choice—but so many businesses exist out there! My cofounder and I researched names for our consultancy business for several months. We eventually decided on the Italian word *abbracci*, which means to hug or embrace. And this idea resonated deeply with us. In HR, we embrace the pain, the human beings, the problems that come up in the workplace. We embrace messy situations and their solutions. We want humanity in the workplace, and this is something we embrace. Oh, and we like to hug!

MONICA: I don't like to hug people. This has been a running joke in the years I've worked with Keri, so that she chose that business name is hilarious. A few years ago, her eight-year-old son told me he was going to teach me how to hug. How perfect! Learning to show an emotional connection with people (and hugging) has been on my development plan. But for her business, I think the name is perfect.

CHECK OUT www.abbraccigroup.com for more information on the business, events, and learning materials as we CHARGE our way towards becoming HR Warriors!

Acknowledgements

Monica

Writing this book has been a fascinating process during which I learned not only about the process of publication but also about the exceptional resources and people needed to create the final product. Now is the chance to extend my gratitude. First and foremost, I am tremendously grateful to God for placing me in the right place, at the right time, to learn and grow as a professional and supplying the necessary backbone to go after my dreams. I am thankful to my parents for consistently telling my siblings and me that there are no limits—that we can accomplish whatever we set ourselves to do. Thank you to Keri Ohlrich and Kelly Guenther for being such strong women and dear friends, setting the example of what an unwavering commitment to success looks like. Thank you to LifeTree Media (the entire team, with special thanks to Maggie Langrick, Sarah Brohman, and Judy Phillips) for taking a chance on previously unpublished authors! Lastly, I have learned a lot from my coworkers, but none more than my first manager, Kurt Haberli, who exemplifies an HR Warrior and whose voice, whenever someone shares a problem with me, I still hear in my head: "Come with a solution, not just a problem!"

Keri

I don't know where to begin to show gratitude. Many thanks to the staff at LifeTree Media for believing in us and making this book 100 percent improved from our first draft. Thank you to our HR peeps who listened to us, read chapters, and gave feedback (Erin Garland, Rileigh Van Driessche, Madeline Borkin, Terry Swarthout, Kelly Guenther, Nandini Basu, Ryan Smith, and Ben Alger, you are all HR Warriors).

And I am grateful for all the mistakes I have made, for the people I have worked with and fought with, and for the situations that make me say "Ugh, I wish I could do that over." Thank you—I learned a tremendous amount!

Now, here come the tears, Monica: girl, wouldn't have done it without you. Thank you for your determination and your belief in what was in my crazy head! To Kelly Guenther, business partner extraordinaire, for believing in the project with your heart and business mind. And—major tears—Steve and Roman, my Scorpios. You always believe that I am a Warrior, even when I am questioning. I am a lucky Libra!

Select Resources

Books

Bennis, Warren G., and Robert J. Thomas. *Geeks & Geezers: How Era, Values, and Defining Moments Shape Leaders.* Boston: Harvard Business School Press, 2002.

Duckworth, Angela. *Grit: Why Passion and Resilience Are the Secrets to Success.* London: Vermilion, 2017.

Ferriss, Timothy. *Tools of Titans: The Tactics, Routines, and Habits of Billionaires, Icons, and World-Class Performers.* New York: Houghton Mifflin Harcourt, 2017.

Fried, Jason, and David Heinemeier Hansson. *Rework.* New York: Crown Business, 2010.

Golomb, Elan. *Trapped in the Mirror: Adult Children of Narcissists in Their Struggle for Self.* New York: Quill, 1995.

Hiatt, Jeff. *ADKAR: A Model for Change in Business, Government, and Our Community.* Loveland, CO: Prosci Learning Center Publications, 2006.

Horowitz, Ben. *The Hard Thing about Hard Things: Building a Business When There Are No Easy Answers.* New York: Harper Business, 2014.

Johnson, Whitney. *Disrupt Yourself: Putting the Power of Disruptive Innovation to Work.* New York: Bibliomotion, 2015.

Laszlo, Christopher. *Sustainable Value: How the World's Leading Companies Are Doing Well by Doing Good.* Sheffield, UK: Greenleaf, 2008.

McGoldrick, Monica, Randy Gerson, and Sueli Petry. *Genograms: Assessment and Intervention.* New York: W.W. Norton, 2008.

Morgan, Gareth. *Images of Organization.* Thousand Oaks, CA: Sage, 2014.

Sandberg, Sheryl, and Nell Scovell. *Lean In: Women, Work, and the Will to Lead.* New York: Alfred A. Knopf, 2017.

Silverman, David. *Interpreting Qualitative Data: Methods for Analyzing Talk, Text and Interaction.* London: Sage, 2011.

Sinek, Simon. *Start with Why: How Great Leaders Inspire Everyone to Take Action.* London: Penguin Books, 2013.

Tannen, Deborah. *You Just Don't Understand: Women and Men in Conversation.* New York: Ballantine Books, 1991.

Trompenaars, Fons, and Charles Hampden-Turner. *Riding the Waves of Culture: Understanding Diversity in Global Business.* London: Nicholas Brealey, 2015.

Magazines

Fast Company
Harvard Business Review
Money
Psychology Today
The Week

Organizations and Media to Follow

ELLEVATE NETWORK: A community of professional women that provides networking events, resources, and connections to help women advance in their careers.

GARTNER: A research and advisory company that delivers content and resources through webinars, podcasts, articles, and e-books to educate and support the HR profession and organizations.

I4CP (INSTITUTE FOR CORPORATE PRODUCTIVITY): A human capital research and data company that helps organizations better anticipate, adapt, and act in a changing business environment.

TED TALKS: Short, powerful talks by educators, business leaders, and influencers, covering a variety of educational topics.

Blogs/E-newsletters

Michael Hyatt—https://michaelhyatt.com: An author, professional coach, and business leader who provides a magazine, a newsletter, books, and resources to those seeking professional development.

LinkedIn Talent Blog—https://business.linkedin.com/talent-solutions/blog: A blog dedicated to the recruiting industry, offering tips, trends, and information.

About the Authors

MONICA FREDE has worked for several Fortune 500 companies such as ManpowerGroup and Quad/Graphics as an HR strategic consultant and HR manager, and in several start-up ventures as a recruiter and consultant. Her passion lies in influencing the minds and hearts of business leaders about what HR can accomplish. Her areas of expertise include identifying and hiring top talent, change management and organizational design, leadership and management training, employee engagement initiatives, communications, project management, employee relations, employment policies, and reductions in force/outsource management. She attended Marquette University on a full basketball scholarship and earned a BA in Writing-Intensive English. She lives in Nashotah, Wisconsin.

DR. KERI OHLRICH, CEO and cofounder of Abbracci Group, is an outcome-focused senior executive with more than twenty-five years of success in the HR, manufacturing, consumer goods, and consulting industries. Leveraging extensive experience in HR leadership for organizations, she is a valuable asset for companies requiring assistance with business, talent, or HR challenges. Her broad areas of expertise include strategic planning, business development, employee relations, talent management, culture change, conflict management, performance management, organizational development, workshop facilitation, and employee engagement and development. Throughout her career, Keri has held leadership positions at a variety of organizations, ranging from start-up to Fortune 500 companies. In her previous roles, she created and implemented HR processes to support the company, redesigned the talent department that supported twenty-five thousand global employees, was responsible for change management for a new business strategy, and overhauled the Human Resources Department.

Keri obtained her PhD in Human Development and Organizational Systems from Fielding Graduate University. She holds an MS in International Peace and Conflict Resolution from American University, an MS in Global Human Resources from Loyola University Chicago, and a BS in Psychology and Business from Carnegie Mellon University. She lives in Pasadena, California.